In an increasi[ng] [...]
must use all th[e] [...]
of Christ as we advance the kingdom of God, including the ministry of deliverance. *The Biblical Guidebook to Deliverance* is a much-needed nudge to the twenty-first-century church in this regard. Inspired by the Holy Spirit and filled with practical guidelines, sound biblical teaching, and strong testimony, this is a valuable resource for the church today. I have known Randy Clark for many years. He is a true gift to our generation. I strongly recommend this book to all who desire to see the lost, broken, and suffering among us set free.

—Happy Leman
Senior Pastor, Vineyard Church of Central Illinois
Vineyard National Board Member

What makes Dr. Randy Clark's *Biblical Guidebook to Deliverance* so valuable is that very few of us are as "free" as we'd like to be. Recently, while we were hosting Randy at our Embassy Church, one of the attendees (whom I know well) purchased this book, took it home, and randomly opened it up to a page on curses and specific sins. Realizing she had committed some of the things mentioned, she repented and began vomiting and expelling demons. Simultaneously, in the same house, this woman's daughter, who had been bedridden for over a year with severe mental health issues, was instantly healed. For the first time in months she got out of her bed, walked to her mother, and started talking coherently. She previously had been diagnosed professionally as bipolar. She has resumed a normal life and is a very bright academic student. Both mom and daughter shared this testimonial in our church…the place erupted with praise thanks to the Lord!

—DOUG SCHNEIDER
PASTOR, EMBASSY CHURCH
ONTARIO, CANADA

The
BIBLICAL
GUIDEBOOK
to
DELIVERANCE

*

RANDY CLARK, DMin

CHARISMA
HOUSE

Most CHARISMA HOUSE BOOK GROUP products are available at special quantity discounts for bulk purchase for sales promotions, premiums, fund-raising, and educational needs. For details, write Charisma House Book Group, 600 Rinehart Road, Lake Mary, Florida 32746, or telephone (407) 333-0600.

THE BIBLICAL GUIDEBOOK TO DELIVERANCE
   by Randy Clark; edited by Susan Thompson
Published by CHARISMA HOUSE
Charisma Media/Charisma House Book Group
600 Rinehart Road
Lake Mary, Florida 32746
www.charismahouse.com

Unless otherwise noted, all Scripture quotations are taken from the Holy Bible, New International Version®, NIV®. Copyright © 1973, 1978, 1984, 2011 by Biblica, Inc.™ Used by permission of Zondervan. All rights reserved worldwide. www.zondervan.com The "NIV" and "New International Version" are trademarks registered in the United States Patent and Trademark Office by Biblica, Inc.™

Scripture quotations marked KJV are from the King James Version of the Bible.

Cover design by Studio Gearbox
Design Director: Justin Evans

Visit the author's website at www.globalawakening.com.

Library of Congress Cataloging-in-Publication Data:
Clark, Randy, 1952-
  The biblical guidebook to deliverance / by Randy Clark;
edited by Susan Thompson. -- First edition.
      pages cm
  Includes bibliographical references and index.
  ISBN 978-1-62998-036-2 (trade paper : alk. paper) -- ISBN
978-1-62998-037-9 (e-book)
  1. Exorcism. I. Title.
  BV873.E8C53 2015
  235'.4--dc23

                                   2015000530

This publication is translated in Spanish under the title *La guía bíblica para la liberación*, copyright © 2015 by Randy Clark, published by Casa Creación, a Charisma Media company. All rights reserved.

22 23 24 25 26 — 10 9 8 7
Printed in the United States of America

CONTENTS

CONTENTS

FOREWORD

IT IS MY PLEASURE TO INTRODUCE THIS EXCELLENT work by such a beloved and respected, Spirit-anointed teacher and evangelist, Dr. Randy Clark.

This training manual on deliverance from demons is absolutely central to the doctrines and mission of the church. The Bible is explicit that "*the reason* the Son of God appeared was to destroy the devil's works" (1 John 3:8). The reason for Jesus's death, resurrection in power, and ascension onto the throne of the universe was to war against Satan and his angels (demons), and to declare: "Now have come the salvation and the power and the kingdom of our God and the authority of his Messiah." Why? "For the accuser... has been hurled down!" (See Revelation 12:10.)

While heaven and its dwellers are rejoicing at this, the dwellers on the earth are experiencing fear "because the devil has gone down to you! He is filled with fury, because he knows his time is short!" (Rev. 12:12). The devil and his messengers (demons) are desperate to do all the damage they can in the brief time that is allotted to them.

So what does that have to do with Christians—God's "chosen people"? We must "get" the reason the description above was written. Like it or not, we are involved—seriously involved.

If we are true disciples of Jesus, we will do what disciples are *explicitly chosen to do*: "He appointed twelve [= us chosen people] that they might be *with him and that he might send them out to preach [speak by the Spirit] and to have authority ['of Christ'] to drive out demons*" (Mark 3:14–15, emphasis added). This "authority" and mission is not limited to "apostles" but to "those who believe" (Mark 16:17).

This central command to expel demons to us "believers" is very different from our usual routine as Christians: to go to church, get into worship, consume religious information and services, and then go back to our "real job," that is, earning a living. No!

Our core mission from Jesus is to *replicate His mission*: "to destroy the works of the devil" as He did with "authority" to cast out demons.

The book you are about to read, then, does not express some fringe activity of Christian rituals. Just the opposite: according to Jesus Himself, *delivering from demonization is the core mission of the believer.* We receive the authority to do this: (1) in the intimate presence of Jesus, (2) we respond to Jesus's presence with Spirit-inspired utterance: praise and prophecy—an utterly toxic environment for demons, then (3) *we act on the almighty authority,* for which Jesus lived, died, was resurrected, and *now bestows on all of us*—and against the demonic—from the throne of heaven!

This excellent book will guide you in how to receive and apply Jesus's authority against "all who are oppressed by the devil" (Jesus's mission described in Acts 10:38, NKJV).

Just do it! It's your main job! So study this book!

—JON MARK RUTHVEN
PROFESSOR EMERITUS, THEOLOGY
REGENT UNIVERSITY
DOCTOR OF MINISTRY MENTOR
UNITED THEOLOGICAL SEMINARY

INTRODUCTION

I WAS IN BERGEN, NORWAY, CONDUCTING A renewal meeting with one of the key leaders in the renewal movement. As is typical in my meetings, after the message was given we moved into a time of healing prayer ministry. With me on the prayer team that day were three Methodist seminarians who were in their last year of seminary. These men had been trained in a theology that denies the existence of demons, having been taught that "deliverance" issues had a psychological root instead.

At one point we began to pray for a man who had been on disability for twenty-three years because of recurring, severe chest pain. He told us that he was not in pain at that moment but wanted prayer. I began to pray, and nothing happened until I said the words, "In Jesus's name." As soon as those words came out of my mouth he grabbed his chest and doubled over in pain. I turned to the seminarians and said, "Watch this!"

"I break your power and cancel your assignment against this man. I command you to leave this man in Jesus's name."

The man was instantly healed. Not only was that man delivered from an afflicting spirit, but also the three seminarians beside me were delivered at that moment from the incorrect theology of liberalism. When they personally witnessed the power of God delivering this man from an afflicting spirit they were forever changed. They went on to become leaders in the renewal movement in Norway. The man who was delivered of the afflicting spirit went off disability and, five years later, when I met his pastor again and asked how the man was doing, his pastor, Reidar Paulson, told me the man had not had any pain since the prayer for deliverance from the afflicting spirit.

F. F. Bosworth, the twentieth-century healing evangelist, author, and pioneer of modern Pentecostalism, said: "A Spirit-filled and praying Church produces an atmosphere in which it is easy for God to work. This makes it difficult for the devil to interfere. *This atmosphere is the Holy Spirit Himself.* He is more than a match for the devil."[1]

Unfortunately not all the church today is Spirit filled. Beginning in the sixth century the *charismata*, or gifts of the Holy Spirit, lost its place as a vital part of the life of the church and has yet to be fully reinstated. In the midst of this loss confusion arose (and remains) regarding all aspects of the *charismata*. The dual ministries of healing and deliverance have been ensnared in the confusion through the centuries, resulting in a refusal by many to engage in this restorative gift given to us by Jesus Himself.

I personally have experienced this confusion. There was a time when, as a pastor, I did not want to deal with deliverance issues because I had no real reference point from which to understand the ministry of deliverance. Demonic manifestations were disturbing to me, and no one around me had any better idea of how to deal with deliverance than I had. When the need for deliverance first reared its head in my church, it was challenging because I was unprepared. I have learned much over the years since my first exposure to the demonic. But for others, confusion still exists.

You may be among the many in ministry who are where I once was regarding deliverance. You have a "need to know" yet you don't know where to turn. When you are faced with the demonic, you have to walk away, hoping the evil will exit the building and not return.

I believe the church is in a time when the issue of deliverance is no longer an option. I do not believe deliverance was ever optional for the church, but it certainly is not now. Our congregations are assaulted daily by an increasingly godless culture, with both the believer and the unbeliever alike swimming in a sea of New Age and occult activity like the West has not seen for centuries.

It is my great desire to see the entire church awakened afresh to the knowledge that deliverance is a New Testament reality that springs from the compassionate heart of God as revealed in Jesus. Bosworth put it this way:

> How insidiously Satan has worked to hide this glorious fact from the people. He has broadcasted the unscriptural, illogical, and worn-out statement that the age of miracles is past, until he has almost succeeded in eclipsing the compassion of God from the eyes of the world.[2]

The church once understood the *charismata*, and some segments of the church still do. Those who dismiss these vehicles of God's self-revelation, saying they have ceased, are dismissing much of what is most precious and dynamic about a relationship with God.[3]

I believe the ministry of deliverance should be restored to the entire church. God in His great love desires that all His beloved sons and daughters live in freedom, unbound from the schemes of the enemy. Jesus paid for this freedom on the cross. His earthly ministry was a constant demonstration of the authority of God over the devil and his minions. Are we not somehow robbing God of His glory when we hold to a cessationist view of God's continued activity in this world?[4]

Through wrong teaching and theology, the church, especially the evangelical Protestant churches, has become dismissive of evil. As believers in the gospel, how can we realistically relegate evil to the realm of superstition? Why should we think Satan and his demons simply exited the stage of humanity at some point, never to return to harass us again?

We don't need to see a demon behind every bush, but we do need to exercise wisdom in acknowledging evil's existence and activity. We must seek to chart a course that balances healthy skepticism with a willingness to believe—but also resist the urge to camp out in the realm of the intellect at the expense of the spiritual. Evil is not simply an unfortunate by-product of human depravity. It is the work of Satan, and we should not shrink from calling it such.

There was a time in the church when deliverance was a fully functioning part of the rite of baptism.[5] This is described in the scholarly writings of Dom Gregory Dix, an English monk and priest of the Anglican Benedictine community who lived in the early twentieth century. His research into the work of rediscovering the baptismal liturgy of the primitive church notes that "from the time of the Book of Acts up through the period of the early church fathers, the giving of the Holy Spirit, through the laying on of hands, was uniformly practiced as part of the larger meaning of Christian baptism. He showed that the laying on of hands occurred immediately following baptism with water."[6] Dix goes on to point out that by the fifth century, water baptism and baptism in the Holy Spirit had become two separate rituals.

In the third and fourth centuries the church instituted prayers for exorcism as an integral part of preparation for baptism. Evidence of this can be found in the Apostolic Constitutions, dated from AD 375 to 380.[7] A significant number of converts in the early church were coming out of rampant paganism, necessitating some form of deliverance as they renounced their pagan gods and practices and embraced the gospel of Jesus Christ. The rites of exorcism were performed both before baptism and after, depending on when they occurred in church history and the particular branch of the church.

It was not uncommon to see prayers for deliverance offered as new believers came out of the waters of baptism. Both adults and infants were exorcised, after which adults would speak the renunciation of Satan and then profess their faith.

Judaism embraces a host of ritual cleansing practices dating to its earliest recorded history that were designed to prevent the profane from making contact with the sacred. Some Jewish scholars connect the laws of impurity to the Genesis narrative in which mankind came in contact with death at the time of the Fall in the garden. As a result of this original sin, Jews continue to practice various cleansing rituals. In these old covenant practices we see a foreshadowing of the new covenant in Jesus Christ.

Martin Luther included exorcism in the baptismal rites of the early Lutheran Church. His *Little Book of Baptism* included the following: "('The officient shall blow three times under the child's eyes and shall say: "Depart thou unclean spirit...'") at the beginning of the rite and other exorcisms."[8] In 1856 exorcism was relegated to a footnote in the Lutheran baptismal rite and abandoned altogether in 1916.[9] The Lutheran Church of the twenty-first century has reinstated the renunciation of the devil and all his works as part of their baptismal rite; however, historian Ryan C. MacPherson acknowledges the church struggles with the concept of Satan: "Satan is a problematic figure and concept for most moderns, and the rites of the Roman Catholic and Episcopal and Lutheran churches are all clearly struggling to make the figure meaningful in the modern world."[10]

The *Book of Common Prayer* of the Anglican Church, first published in 1549 and most recently updated in 1979, has provided liturgical Protestantism with a structure for worship and daily Christian living.[11] "Holy Baptism" as outlined in the *Book of Common Prayer* includes the rite of exorcism.[12] Brian Cummings, in his exhaustive study of the liturgical church, states this about baptism: "The 1549 *Book of Common Prayer* placed a central emphasis on the verbal promises of faith, but also involved physical actions such as the signing of the forehead and exorcism."[13]

Although some of today's liturgical churches retain exorcism as a part of the celebration of the rite of baptism, for most these rites are, sadly, rote rather than reality. The Catholic Church, more than any other denomination, has historically embraced a holistic paradigm of healing that includes the rite of exorcism, and continues to practice exorcism in the twenty-first century.

The paradigm of deliverance as part of the ministry of healing needs to be restored to the entire church, across all denominational lines, if we are to deal effectively with the plethora of issues facing us in this century. As the bride of Christ we must link arms and take an unflinching stand against Satan and his minions.

What little our culture seems to know about deliverance comes largely from the entertainment industry.

From the *The Exorcist* (1973) to *The Rite* (2011) Hollywood has dramatized the role of exorcism. Evil is a lucrative and marketable commodity—and a fascinating one. The image of deliverance as some bizarre match between the devil and an unwitting human has gone a long way toward reinforcing the cultural context in which we find this ministry today in the church.

Deliverance scholar Dr. Arlin Epperson[14] estimates that 95 percent of churches in America do not understand the need for deliverance ministry. Of the 5 percent that do, only about 1 percent are willing to engage in it. He has seen cases in which 50 percent of the congregation leave when pastors begin ministering in spiritual gifts, deliverance, and inner healing.

Although deliverance ministry is unpredictable by its very nature, not all deliverances involve confrontations such as those depicted in *The Exorcist* or *The Rite*. Often deliverance resembles the ministry of inner healing, during which people are set free without disruption by the demonic. With proper training, deliverance can proceed quietly and respectfully to assist those who struggle with demonic beings, principalities, and powers beyond their control. When unusual and disturbing manifestations occur, patience, persistence, and knowledge of the dynamics of deliverance are needed.

The model we use in deliverance is loving, non-humiliating, and pastoral. It is based on the one developed and used effectively by Pablo Bottari to minister to thousands.[15] Just as Jesus came to set the captives free, we too are called to minister in the power of the Spirit to those who are demonized. It is truly a wonderful thing to see someone set free from the demonic. What joy when chains are broken and people can begin to live in the fullness of life that God intends for them.

I went through a period of five years, while in college and then seminary, when I ceased to believe in demons because of the liberal teaching I was sitting under. My malleable young mind embraced the views and theology that said any manifestation of evil in a person was rooted in mental illness. In the same way that much of the Western church embraces the rationalistic worldview that discounts the supernatural, I thought Jesus was condescending to the first-century worldview of mental illness. I eventually saw the error of this kind of teaching, but many believers have not. The church is not moving in its full power because of our dismissive attitude toward evil.

Our views on evil and deliverance can change quite quickly when we come face-to-face with the demonic. This happened to two Baptist seminary professors. A young, petite woman weighing less than 110 pounds came into their office one day for counseling. During the session she began to manifest demonically. Even though she was very petite, because of the demonic supernatural strength that was manifesting through her, she almost succeeded in tearing up their office before they were able to get her under control. She had a dis-embodied, malevolent spirit with a will and intellect of its own at work within her. This experience was a game changer for these two professors. Unable to explain this woman's behavior with secular psychology, they decided it was time to learn about deliverance. Both of these men had doctoral degrees. One's father was a psychiatrist and the other was over the pastoral care department of the Baptist seminary in Buenos Aires, Argentina.

Many leaders in the church today must walk a fine line regarding deliverance. For the sake of legitimacy, they tend to default to secular psychology with a veneer of Christianese when dealing with the demonic. That is all well and good until you actually encounter a demon. The first time a demon talked to me, that type of blended theology went out the window.

There are a number of books on the subject of deliverance that I would recommend. Francis MacNutt's *Deliverance From Evil Spirits*[16] and Neal Lozano's *Unbound*[17] are excellent resources, as is James Goll's

Deliverance From Darkness: The Essential Guide to Defeating Demonic Strongholds and Oppression.[18] Those of you seeking an authoritative overview of deliverance from the perspective of the medical and psychiatric fields, written from a conservative Christian biblical perspective, might want to read the Reverend Malachi Martin's *Hostage to the Devil: The Possession and Exorcism of Five Contemporary Americans.*[19] The book came out of a symposium at Notre Dame University in 1976 for a gathering of anthropologists, psychologists, psychiatrists, those in the medical field, social workers, and biblical scholars. It is not for the faint of heart. A Jesuit priest and professor, Father Martin was an exorcist for thirty years in the Catholic church.

This book you are about to read focuses on what we call "ground-level spiritual warfare," which deals with the demonic as it impacts individuals. There is another level of spiritual warfare called "strategic-level spiritual warfare," which deals with principalities and powers over areas, cities, regions, and countries. Theologian Walter Wink, in his trilogy of books on the subject,[20] refers to this second level of demonic activity as "structural evil." One problem I have with Walter Wink's view is that he implies all demonic activity is structural evil. I don't agree with him. Wink's view regarding structural evil rules out the existence of personal demonic powers known as powers and principalities. This liberal viewpoint has some truth to it, but it is not the total reality regarding the evil realm of the demonic, powers, rulers, and principalities.

There are many examples of structural evil throughout history. Take for example the Cambodian Civil War (1969–1975) that resulted in the deaths of more than one million Cambodians in the killing fields of Pol Pot. This is a brutal picture of structural evil, which resulted in hideous genocide. Soldiers threw babies in the air, using them for target practice as their mothers watched, while others took infants and slammed their heads against trees.[21] This abhorrent behavior is an example of evil that influenced an entire people group. It manifested by means of demonic powers and principalities that influence the philosophy of a culture, causing people to think a certain way so the power of the state is actualized by its people.

Adolf Hitler's Nazi Germany is another horrifying example of structural evil. More than twelve million people were exterminated in the Holocaust. The largest people group of the twelve million were Jews, but the dead also included other people groups considered "undesirable" by Hitler and his regime.

Hitler's commitment to the occult strongly influenced his ideology and that of Nazi Germany. It was the occultic Thule Society that gave birth to the German Workers' Party and the German Socialist Party, both of which eventually became the National Socialist German Worker Party of Nazi Germany. Dietrich Eckart, a committed occultist and member of the Thule Society at its highest levels, exerted tremendous influence over Hitler, taking him from obscurity to the head of Nazi Germany through training in esoteric occult lodges prevalent in Germany at the turn of the century.[22] These occult societies had their roots in Tibetan Buddhism.[23]

Although structural evil is not a focus of this book, I believe it is important that we are aware of the distinction when dealing with deliverance. Ground-level deliverance issues such as those we encounter in most deliverance situations in churches and in ministry do not involve strategic-level spiritual warfare. Those ministering deliverance should avoid attempts to displace regional principalities and powers unless they are led of the Holy Spirit to engage on that level and are specifically trained in that type of warfare.

While ministering in Argentina I have had the privilege to work alongside many church leaders who practice strategic-level spiritual warfare. I have interviewed them and others from around the world on the subject. Although I do not feel I have been called to rebuke Satan or his principalities, I know that other believers have been authorized by Scripture or by the Holy Spirit to do so.

In the course of my research I have discovered there is a broad diversity of opinion about how this type of spiritual warfare should be practiced and by whom. Some teach that this kind of prayer is only for the most spiritual, most holy people in the church. Others say there is an anointing for it, given by the Holy Spirit, and that even children may have the anointing. Some say if you are called to engage in warfare on this level, then there first needs to be spiritual unity among the pastors involved and preparatory actions such as identificational repentance.

My friend John Paul Jackson has written a book on this subject, titled *Needless Casualties of War*.[24] Though I agree with much in the book, nowhere does it deal with those who are called to engage in strategic-level spiritual warfare and do it wisely. Is it dangerous? Yes. Is it forbidden? No—but it definitely is not for the average Christian. It should be the domain of those invited into it by the Holy Spirit, who are living in holiness, and whose faith for the battle is supplied by the Holy Spirit.

It is my desire in writing this book that you, as a believer, gain a better understanding of deliverance as part of the church's heritage and as an integral part of the ministry of healing today. And that, as a result, you are encouraged to help restore the ministry of deliverance to the church.

You will find here a practical guide to ministering deliverance based on a foundation of love and respect. "For God so loved the world that he gave his one and only Son" (John 3:16). When the Word became flesh, light came into the world. This light shines in the darkness and will not be extinguished. Jesus, the light of the world, came to bind up the brokenhearted and set the captives free (Luke 4:18).

He is still doing this work today through His bride, the church. We must encourage one another to lay aside all hindrances so the church may enter more completely into the work of fulfilling the Great Commission in our time. If we are to understand the fullness of the Great Commission and emphasize what the Bible emphasizes, then we need to understand that the authority delegated to us by Jesus encompasses deliverance as well as physical healing.

There was a time when I did not believe what I wrote in the preceding paragraph. What brought about the change in my theology and practice regarding demons is the subject of our next chapter.

Chapter 1

MY INTRODUCTION TO DELIVERANCE

◆━━◆◆◆◆◆◆◆◆━━◆

I HAD BEEN A PASTOR FOR FOURTEEN YEARS when I encountered my first demon. At the time I was pastoring a Baptist church. We had invited a team from the Vineyard to come minister at our church, and during their visit we experienced a powerful move of the Holy Spirit. Sometime earlier a woman evangelist was ministering at a nearby Assemblies of God church. Having heard that manifestations of the presence of the Holy Spirit occurred when this woman preached, I wanted to see for myself what was going on. Hoping not to be noticed or seen, I sat on the back row. I like to joke that I had on sunglasses and a trench coat, but I didn't. I was just sitting there on the back row hoping no one would notice me because it wasn't a good thing for a Baptist pastor to be interested in manifestations of the Spirit.

At one point during her teaching a large man got up, roaring, making noises, and growling. As his behavior got out of control, four men tackled him, one on each limb. They were screaming at him and he was yelling, hitting, and sweating. He got up and tried to run, and they tackled him again. They wouldn't let him get away; they were wrestling with him. It was a classic deliverance scene, American style, and it made me think I didn't want anything to do with deliverance. Then this guy started vomiting. I'm not a fan of vomiting, so that really sealed the deal for me.

I believe a lot of the behavior we see during deliverance is nothing more than manifestations of cultural expectations. In our limited knowledge as a culture we expect chaos and things such as vomiting when someone is experiencing deliverance. Other cultures have different expectations. Koreans don't vomit. They burp—because that is what they believe is supposed to happen when demons come out of a person. Bottari teaches that vomiting and the like is not necessary to deliver people of demons. His ten-step model for deliverance is found in his book *Free in Christ*.[1]

A VISITATION OF THE HOLY SPIRIT

My second encounter with the demonic occurred in my own church. As I mentioned earlier, we experienced a visitation from the Holy Spirit when we hosted a team from the Vineyard at our church. During their ministry a demon manifested in a woman. Because the Vineyard team was small, consisting of only five people, and was ministering to hundreds who were at the meeting, the team tried to shut down the demonic manifestation rather than deal with it. It was unfortunate that such a teachable moment was lost.

My friend and fellow pastor Mike Hutchings was there when this Holy Spirit visitation occurred. He was the pastor of a sister Baptist church in the area. Also in attendance was John Crone from another nearby American Baptist Church. The three of us were good friends. Once a year the American Baptist Churches of the Great Rivers Region would give an award to a pastor of note from one of the 242 churches in their region. John had received the award in 1982, my church received it for evangelism in 1983, and Mike's church received one in 1984. Being recognized with the award is a big deal and was a good thing for each of us. Winners, in effect, climb the denominational ladder. One of the benefits is that you can be considered for denominational positions.

We might have been award winners, but Mike, John, and I essentially fell off the ladder after the Holy Spirit visitation. In John's church people started falling down—coming under the influence of the Holy Spirit, or being "slain in the Spirit." That was something new, and no one knew what was going on. Some people thought they were witnessing heart attacks and called 911. Because of it all John eventually agreed to leave his church.

I came under fire at my church as well. The leader of our denomination for our area came to assess the situation. Perhaps he seized the opportunity to discredit this move of the Holy Spirit because our denomination was hostile to the gifts of the Spirit, or perhaps it was just unfortunate, but those he talked with were the ones who had less than favorable experiences. Many people had wonderful experiences, but he somehow missed them. There was a move to oust me, and even though it did not succeed, I eventually left on my own because I came to understand that I didn't belong in that denomination anymore.

The Lord had spoken to me about going to another city to start a new church. My leaving put the wheels in motion for a move to St. Louis, Missouri, where I did start a new church, which I pastored for sixteen years. John was actually fired, not because of anything he did, but simply because he was my friend. Because denominational leaders lacked the knowledge and training to understand demonization and healing, they instead reacted out of fear and ignorance.

One night I was driving home from a James Robison Bible conference with several deacons. In the car on the way home that night we tried to process what we had seen. With a seventeen-hour drive ahead of us, we decided to listen to some of John Wimber's teaching series on tape. John was the leader of the Vineyard, a network of churches that helped to pioneer the introduction of healing and deliverance into the evangelical churches.

One of the tapes dealt with deliverance. It was a bit graphic, and just listening to it convinced me more than ever that I didn't want to deal with the demonic. Little did I know that I would soon face a demon for the first time in my own ministry.

SURPRISED BY THE DEMONIC

Having returned from the trip, I was scheduled to meet with a fellow pastor who had recently learned he had a terminal illness. Word had gotten out that after the Vineyard team's visit my church was experiencing healings, and this dear man wanted prayer for his own healing. I met him accompanied by four or five people from my church, and we prayed for him. It was close to midnight when we finished, and he went home. One of our prayer team members, Alan,[2] asked if we would pray for him before we wrapped up for the night. He had just started a successful new business and wanted prayers for God to bless him in the midst of his new-found success.

Alan had been a member of my church for several years. He was in leadership but had experienced a false conversion. The night the Vineyard team came to our church, Alan was gloriously saved. He was touched so powerfully by the Holy Spirit that he thought he was going to die. He asked the Lord to stay His hand because he couldn't take any more. As a result of this powerful touch from God, Alan was given a gift of discernment of spirits.

As the team and I prayed for Alan, one of the women on the team began to manifest demonically. It was as if somebody had popped her with an uppercut to the chin. She literally came off her feet, flew backward, and landed on the floor, where she remained while she hit her head repeatedly on the floor and made strange motions with her hands. This woman was a leader in our church with a position of high visibility and a heart of concern. I viewed her as a pillar in the church; yet there she was, flopping around on the floor, banging her head and flailing her arms.

I did not know what to do. To say I was unprepared is an understatement. The sum total of my training in deliverance consisted of the one Wimber tape I'd recently listened to; one chapter I had read from a book on deliverance by Francis MacNutt, a former Catholic priest and a Charismatic Renewal pioneer; and what I had seen at the Assemblies of God church some time earlier.

Not knowing what else to do, we stopped praying, and Alan and I walked over to look at her. I am not exaggerating when I tell you that Alice's face was almost unrecognizable. In a matter of seconds, fluid had formed in the tissues of her face. Her neck had swollen to the size of her head. Her eyes rolled in different directions as she continued to bang her head on the floor. We put a pillow under her head, and the banging stopped temporarily.

I went over to the platform and sat down, dumbfounded. Alan came over and said to me, "You know what we've got here, don't you?" I knew next to nothing about deliverance, but I knew enough to be certain that we didn't want the demons talking to us. I told Alan not to say that she had a demon. Before we could say anything else, Alice started slamming her head on the floor again. Alan and I went back and stood on each side of her. It was bizarre to see the demonic manifesting in her. Her eyes went to Alan, and she said in a deep guttural voice, "You're ugly, I hate you!" Now we had a demon talking to us!

At that point in my ministry I didn't understand the authority I carried from the finished work of Jesus on the cross. I was grasping for a method, but without the knowledge of my authority, I was essentially bluffing. And frankly I was scared. I was actually freaked out by the whole experience.

I started commanding the demon to come out in the name of Jesus, but it knew I lacked confidence in my authority, and it wouldn't leave. After commanding it a few more times I started to threaten it, but that didn't work either. Then I started yelling at it. And Alan started yelling at it, and so did Alice's husband. We were angry that this demon wasn't coming out, and her husband was very upset to see his wife in such a state. We got louder and louder until we finally realized that loudness and authority weren't going hand in hand. Often such abrasive tactics will stir up a demon, causing greater trauma to the demonized person, but we didn't know that.

Grasping at straws, I went to the pulpit, retrieved the anointing oil I kept there, put some on my hand, and made the sign of the cross on her forehead with the oil just like I'd seen in *The Exorcist*. I'm not making this up. I actually did that. But it didn't make any difference. I took the big brass cross from the communion table and laid it across her body. That made no difference either. I was at a loss. Then I remembered that Blaine Cook's wife, Becky, successfully ministered to people who were demonized. She moved in authority in that realm. Blaine was the teacher with the Vineyard team that had recently visited our church. Desperate, we tried to call Becky in California. Strangely, though, my office phone was dead, and the other phone, in the education building, was dead too.

We asked Betty, one of the team members, to go home and call Blaine. Betty's husband, like many in our church, was not entirely comfortable with the visitation of the Holy Spirit we had experienced with the Vineyard team—especially the deliverance aspect. The Vineyard team had apologized for not having the time to train us properly in deliverance and had promised to return for further training. They had cautioned us not to attempt deliverance until we were trained. For these reasons Betty's husband didn't want her involved—until he learned that the woman in need of deliverance was the wife of his best friend!

Together they called Becky Cook. She gave Betty five steps to walk through with Alice, as well as the authority to minister the deliverance. Because a sexual element is often present during demonic activity, there is wisdom in having women minister to women and men to men.

Betty was able to walk Alice through the five steps without any yelling or shouting. Speaking quietly and moving confidently in authority, she asked Alice to open her eyes. Betty knew that she needed to address Alice, not the demon. At first the demon kept saying, "No!" when Betty would ask to talk to Alice. Eventually we could see in Alice's eyes that the demon was no longer in control of her personality. The eyes are very revealing of what is going on in deliverance.

After Betty began to address Alice directly, she was able to determine the root cause of the demonic infestation. Awful things that had happened to Alice had caused a well of unforgiveness to form in her life. When she was able to renounce the pain and unforgiveness, it appeared that she had been set free. We prayed for her to be healed in the Spirit—and to be filled with the Spirit, as the Scripture instructs (Eph. 5:18), so the place left vacant by the departing demon cannot be filled with seven more that are more wicked than the original. We believed by faith that the deliverance was successful, and because it was 3:00 a.m., we sent her home. That was Saturday night.

LEARNING HOW TO SET PEOPLE FREE

Sunday morning her husband met me at the church with a look of frenzy. Alice was worse. She became suicidal upon returning home, and her husband had to hide all the knives in the house and take their children to stay with grandparents. Our experiences the prior evening had created enough faith in me that I felt confident in our authority to deal with this a second time. I was actually a bit excited about the opportunity to try this again, having seen how the demon responded to the authority in Betty the night before.

Because I knew deliverance was a very problematic topic in our church, I asked Alice's husband to bring her back to church that evening. I didn't want anyone else present besides a few deacons and myself. Knowing I was going to be involved in deliverance that night, I preached on the passage in Colossians 2:15 where God made a public spectacle of the demons, triumphing over them. I even confided in one of my deacons about the impending deliverance. He was with me that night during the deliverance but was so freaked out that he held his Bible out in front of him the whole time.

That evening the deacons and I walked Alice through deliverance. What had taken three hours the night before was accomplished in less than half an hour that night. There were a total of eight personalities infesting Alice, each with a name. We had cast one out the first night, but seven had remained. I wrote down the names of each because I knew nobody would remember all of that, and because I wanted to make sure the experience was real—that she wasn't trying to fake the whole thing. We were able to set her free, and afterward she asked if I would baptize her again. She felt it was necessary.

I'm not in favor of rebaptizing people, but Alice felt so cleansed, so free, so changed by this experience that she wanted to be baptized again. I agreed and went through the process with her. As she came up out of the water I realized that she was now "drunk in the Spirit." She fell on the floor and remained there, laughing hysterically for a while. We had prayed for her to be filled with the Holy Spirit, and she had definitely been filled.

I have seen this type of holy laughter in Toronto and when I was a little boy. At times my grandmother in our Baptist church would just laugh and laugh. Everything was funny to her. In the late 1950s they didn't call it "holy laughter." It was called "getting happy." Alice was set free, and she has been free ever since. But that's not the end of the story.

Alice had a cousin, a woman in her thirties, who had epilepsy and suffered from frequent grand mal seizures that were so severe they caused brain damage. Because of the teaching Alice and her husband had received from the Vineyard team, that God still heals today, and because of Alice's own healing, they went to pray for her cousin. The moment they began to pray, the cousin went into a grand mal seizure. Thinking it might be a demon, they called me for advice. I was hesitant to see it that way, so I suggested they wait a week or so, return and pray again, and see if the same thing happened. They did, and the same thing happened: the cousin went into a grand mal seizure the moment they began to pray. Since we were pretty sure we were dealing with the demonic, we set up a deliverance session. Alice and her husband requested that Alan minister with us.

That was my first scheduled deliverance session, and the devil started to mess with me. He told me it was a setup and that I would make a public spectacle of myself when I tried to deliver her. He said she would have another seizure and that he was going to kill her, or at the very least cause more brain damage. I became very nervous. It was quite intense. I began reading up. I read MacNutt again, and I listened to Wimber's tape again.

I arrived first at the session, followed by Alan, who drove up in his new car, got out, slammed the door, and said: "Praise the Lord! Hallelujah!" I was taken aback. Being a Baptist, it would take me a year to learn to raise one hand and another year before I could raise both hands in praise. I didn't think Alan was taking this whole thing seriously enough. Wasn't he aware that the enemy could be setting us up?

We began the session quietly, sitting down with Alice's cousin and gently explaining to her that we wouldn't be shouting and doing all that nonsense like she might have seen on TV or in the movies. Instead we would take authority, pray over her, and if the demonic was present, we would set her free. It seemed like a good and reasonable start. Alan and I then excused ourselves and drew away for a few minutes of preparatory prayer. Everything seemed nicely under control. That lasted all of ten seconds before the woman fell off her seat, hit the floor, and began manifesting.

We immediately went back to her, and Alan took the lead. He spoke to the demons and said, "I know all about you!" I thought he was speaking to the woman, and I was surprised that he would say such a thing. How could he know all about this woman? My mind was racing and I was thinking that perhaps Alan was going crazy. We had been warned that when someone gets involved in ministering deliverance there is a chance that person could go crazy. I thought maybe it had happened to Alan. Then he said, "I know what happened. I know your names. I know there are two demons in you and you have to come out." And then he named the demons and commanded them to come out in Jesus's name.

As Alan spoke to the demons, the woman began to rear up and spit and scream. It was crazy. And then Alan said, "I know all about Mike." At the mention of the name "Mike" the woman lost it and began to manifest even more. Then Alan said, "And I know about Benton." That was the name of a town a few miles from our church. The woman lost it again. Then Alan told her he knew about the adultery, and even though she denied it, Alan kept insisting that God had told him "adultery." At this point the woman told us it was her husband who had committed adultery in the garage with a teenage girl just a week earlier. She wanted to get a shotgun and kill him. Alan apologized for the misinterpretation.

Then Alice took Alan aside and told him the real story. Mike had raped her cousin twenty-three years ago, at the age of sixteen, in Benton. Only Alice and her aunt knew about the rape. Her aunt had told her daughter never to speak to anyone about this again. Alan returned to the woman and was able to minister to her. He walked her through forgiveness and the other necessary steps, and commanded the demons to leave her. At that moment both Alan and I heard the swinging doors at the back of the church screech, as if the demons were exiting the building. Alice's cousin had been set free.

A NEW BIBLICAL PERSPECTIVE

During the deliverance session, after Alan had mentioned Mike and Benton, Alice said to him, "I've got to talk to you!" They stepped aside, and Alice asked Alan, "How do you know these things? No one knows about her being raped by Mike in Benton but myself and her mother." He told Alice and me that he had seen it all in a full-blown vision. He went on to tell us that the night before, while he was sleeping, he had suddenly felt a hand on his throat, choking him. He felt as if he was being strangled. Something was choking him, and he kept trying to say, "Jesus!" but he couldn't get the word out. When he finally managed to say the name of Jesus, the thing left. At that point God took him into an open vision. He saw a young woman of sixteen being raped by a man named Mike in the back of a car. He knew the make and color of the car. He saw the street sign where the car was parked and the little sign at the entrance to the city, with the name *Benton* on it.

God told him there was witchcraft from the Cherokee nation involved and that her grandfather had been a shaman. He had taken her into caves and would tell her that the spirits of wind and fire would protect her. He had involved her in shamanistic things. I was amazed the Holy Spirit had revealed all of that to Alan.

Later when I shared this deliverance experience with John Wimber, his response surprised me. He told me that the actual deliverance was the easy part; the harder part was helping people acclimate back into a normal lifestyle. He said it usually is necessary to walk them through a lengthy reintegration process because so many social skills have been impaired by the warped demonic reality they had been living under. Many people who have been delivered find it necessary to relearn acceptable behaviors and often test those close to them to see how unconditional their love is.

After these experiences my eyes were opened to the biblical reality of the demonic. I no longer had any doubt that the devil was real and that demons are real, malevolent spirits with a will and an intellect that can affect people. As a result I shifted from a secular, naturalistic, psychological interpretation of demons to what I call a truly biblical perspective.

Let's turn our attention now to take a brief look at Satan as he is mentioned in the Old Testament and as the defeated foe of Jesus in the New Testament.

Chapter 2

DELIVERANCE: A NEW
TESTAMENT REALITY

◆◆━━◆◆◆◆◆━━◆◆

THE DEVIL AND HIS DEMONS
IN THE OLD TESTAMENT

THE OLD TESTAMENT PERSPECTIVE OF SATAN IS that he is a deceiver, the enemy of God's people who tempts them to sin against God, especially by presumption. He is also portrayed as the accuser of the people of God, both in the Book of Job and in passages in Zechariah. The word *devil* is not found in the Old Testament, only *Satan*. There are indications that the writers of the Old Testament, which was written in the context of polytheism (the belief in many gods), struggled not to emphasize the role of Satan lest this personality would in some way threaten the monotheism (one God) they were fighting to establish in the minds of the Israelites. As a result, we find very little about Satan in the Old Testament.

The major passages relating to Satan in the Old Testament are found in 1 Chronicles 21:1, Job 1:6–2:7, and Zechariah 3:1. Other passages that have been connected to Satan, though he is not named in them, are Genesis 3:1–19, in which the serpent that tempted Eve is identified as Satan; Isaiah 14:12–15, which some commentators see as a reference to Satan and others as a reference to the king of Tyre, who represents the Antichrist; and Ezekiel 28:12–19, which commentators believe refers to the king of Tyre.

THE NEW TESTAMENT PERSPECTIVE OF SATAN

The name *Satan* is found thirty-three times in the New Testament, and *devil* is found thirty-three times. Unlike in the Old Testament where Satan is an undefeated enemy, the New Testament reveals Satan as a defeated foe. The head of the great serpent is crushed under the heel of believers to whom the power of the Spirit is made available in Christ.[1] In the Book of Romans Paul makes it quite clear that "we are more than conquerors through him who loved us. For I am convinced that neither death nor life, neither angels nor demons... will be able to separate us from the love of God that is in Christ Jesus our Lord."[2]

The New Testament writers make no bones in identifying Satan for who he is. Matthew refers to the devil as Beelzebul, the prince of demons.[3] The apostle John says he is the father of lies,[4] and one who disguises himself as an angel of light.[5] In the Book of Acts Satan deceives Ananias and Sapphira, trapping them in a lie that costs them their lives.[6] Paul also identifies those who serve Satan as ones who masquerade as servants of righteousness.[7]

In Ephesians Paul says Satan is the ruler of the kingdom of the air and the spirit who is now at work in those who are disobedient.[8] This title gives insight into the devil's role. Because he is not omnipresent, he must rely upon his hierarchy of evil, the demonic realm, to bring about this disobedience. In Acts Paul addresses the issue of magicians whom we would today call shamans, and identifies them as those in whom the devil is at work.[9] Shamans and those involved in witchcraft and the occult are the enemies of all righteousness, full of deceit and villainy, and try to pervert the righteous ways of God. They do everything they can to turn people away from faith or belief in Jesus as Savior and Lord. From the standpoint of deliverance, it is important to understand who these people are and how they operate.

In Acts 13:4–12 Paul relates one of the many power encounters between the servant of God and the servant of the devil found in the Bible. The Jewish sorcerer, Bar-Jesus, who is attempting to stop Barnabas and Saul from sharing the gospel with the proconsul, is blinded by the hand of the Lord. When the proconsul sees the power of God on display, he is astonished at the teaching of the Lord and believes. Notice too that Bar-Jesus is one of the false prophets that we are warned about in the Scriptures.[10]

On my first trip to Mozambique to work with Iris Ministries founders Rolland and Heidi Baker, I saw the most influential witch doctor in the region delivered from demons. He had seen Jesus heal so many people through Rolland and Heidi's ministry that, like Simon the sorcerer in Acts 8,[11] he wanted the power he saw in Jesus. He understood spiritual power and wanted to switch sides. He realized the powers he had been working with were no match for the power of the Holy Spirit in the name of Jesus.

At his request team members led him in a prayer of repentance. Confessing his sins and acknowledging Jesus as his Lord and Savior, he was set free. As the man burned his fetishes, the woman he was living with was healed instantly of deafness.

In his second letter to the church in Corinth, Paul says Satan will attempt to outwit us because we are unaware of his schemes.[12] He calls him the "god of this age" who "has blinded the minds of unbelievers, so that they cannot see the light of the gospel that displays the glory of Christ."[13] Paul is also highlighting the necessity of forgiveness as a way to prevent Satan from outwitting us, noting that "we are not unaware of his schemes."

The writer of Hebrews refers to Satan as "him who holds the power of death—that is, the devil."[14] In 2 Timothy Paul portrays Satan as one who sets traps in order to take people captive to his will.[15] Peter warns believers: "Be alert and of sober mind. Your enemy the devil prowls around like a roaring lion looking for someone to devour."[16] In his first letter to the church in Corinth Paul gives specific instructions to believers to help them understand what it means to exercise self-control in their marriages[17] and to be alert to those who worship idols.[18]

The first three Gospels, called the Synoptic Gospels because their accounts are so parallel to one another, present a strong emphasis upon Jesus's victory over the devil and his demons. In Matthew, Mark, and Luke we see Jesus's victory over the devil's temptations during His forty days in the desert immediately after His baptism.[19] Luke records Jesus healing a woman who was bound by Satan for eighteen years,[20] and tells of the seventy who returned rejoicing that the demons submitted in Jesus's name.[21] Mark tells of Jesus casting a demon out of a possessed man after the demon identifies Jesus by name.[22] A little later on Mark tells the dramatic story of Jesus healing the Gerasene demoniac.[23]

In the Book of Acts Peter speaks at Cornelius's house, declaring the power of God in Jesus to heal and deliver all who were under the power of the devil.[24] In Ephesians Paul addresses two issues that are very pertinent to the ministry of deliverance.

The first is the issue of forgiveness,[25] which is crucial to healing and deliverance—and which we will address more fully in a later chapter. The second is a point of instruction to believers about how to be equipped to take a stand against the devil's schemes.[26] It is here that Paul tells us our struggle is not against flesh and blood but against the rulers, authorities, powers of the dark world, and spiritual forces of evil in the heavenly realms. Here Paul is also giving us insight into the hierarchy of evil.

The apostle John is very clear to identify Satan as the one implicit in the death of Jesus, calling him a "murderer from the beginning"[27] and identifying him as the one who entered Judas Iscariot to betray Jesus.[28] John saw the great battle in heaven between Michael and his angels and the dragon and his angels: "But he was not strong enough, and they lost their place in heaven. The great dragon was hurled down—that ancient serpent called the devil, or Satan, who leads the whole world astray...He seized the dragon, that ancient serpent, who is the devil, or Satan, and bound him for a thousand years."[29]

The New Testament is rich with teaching on Satan. There is far too much in it to be covered here. By now, however, you should have both a firm understanding that under the new covenant the devil is a defeated foe and a clear understanding of who Satan and his demons are. With this basic biblical understanding, let's examine the theological aspects of deliverance.

Chapter 3

THE THEOLOGY OF DELIVERANCE

———————

EACH ONE OF US IS A BODY, SOUL, AND SPIRIT, created as a spirit being. It is our spirits that connect us with God. When anyone asks Jesus Christ to come into their life, God's Spirit connects with their spirit, and they are joined with Jesus. God's Spirit bears witness with our spirits that we are children of God (Rom. 8:16). When sin separates us from God, our spirits still function, but because the spirit was designed to connect and relate to God, sin causes it to separate from God.

The soul is also a part of our inner man. It comprises the mind, which gives us our capacity to think; the will, which is our capacity to choose; and emotions, which are our capacity to feel. Our bodies are the temples of the Holy Spirit, and they give us our physical identity and enable us to relate to the physical world.

At the time of our salvation we are totally redeemed— body, soul, and spirit. The spirit is fully redeemed as

God's Spirit connects with ours. The soul, comprised of our mind, will, and emotions, is also redeemed. First Corinthians 2:16 says that we have the mind of Christ. Philippians 2:13 says that God is in us to will and work for His good pleasure. In other words, God gives us the desire and the power to do His will. He redeems our emotions with the fruit of His Spirit, which is love, joy, peace, patience, kindness, goodness, gentleness, faithfulness, and self-control (Gal. 5:22–23).

DELIVERANCE: THE CHILDREN'S BREAD

What has been redeemed in us must be reclaimed. Since God's Spirit indwells our spirits, I believe our spirits have been fully reclaimed, but the soul must be reclaimed as well. This is what the apostle Paul was teaching in 2 Corinthians 4:16: "Therefore we do not lose heart. Though outwardly we are wasting away, yet inwardly we are being renewed day by day."

Deliverance is the "children's bread" Jesus referred to in Matthew 15:26. It's an integral part of the atonement and central to the ministry of healing that He entrusted to His church. Deliverance, as New Testament reality, flows from the finished work of the Cross. Jesus was not defeated on the cross by Satan. Quite the contrary; He defeated the devil when He rose from the dead: "And having disarmed the powers and authorities, he made a public spectacle of them, triumphing over them by the cross" (Col. 2:15).

We now have a new covenant of hope as we behold our risen Savior, seated at the right hand of God with all things under His feet. Let us hear with our spiritual ears and eyes Paul's prayer of praise and thanksgiving:

> I pray also that the eyes of your heart may be enlightened in order that you may know the hope to which he has called you, the riches of his glorious inheritance in his holy people, and his incomparably great power for us who believe. That power is the same as the mighty strength he exerted when he raised Christ from the dead and seated him at his right hand in the heavenly realms, far above all rule and authority, power and dominion, and every name that is invoked, not only in the present age but also in the one to come. And God placed all things under his feet and appointed him to be head over everything for the church, which is his body, the fullness of him who fills everything in every way.
>
> —EPHESIANS 1:18–23

Paul follows this passage with an explanation of the steps God will take to accomplish His purpose, beginning with the salvation of individuals. Those who were once dead in sin can become alive in Christ. "And God raised us up with Christ and seated us with him in the heavenly realms in Christ Jesus, in order that in the coming ages he might show the incomparable riches of his grace" (Eph. 2:6–7). We now stand in the place of victory with Christ, and it includes victory over the demonic.

OUR KINGDOM AUTHORITY

We never see Jesus wrestling or struggling with demonic powers. He always acts from a position of authority, manifesting the Father's kingdom. He told the multitude: "But if I drive out demons by the finger of God, then the kingdom of God has come to you" (Luke 11:20). He simply commands the demons to come out, using the authority He has from the Father, which the demons have to obey. "All the people were amazed and said to each other, 'What words are these? With authority and power he gives orders to evil spirits and they come out!'" (Luke 4:36).

As believers standing in victory with Christ, we too have this authority. Jesus has commissioned us to go into the world with His good news, telling us that miracles, signs, and wonders will accompany us (Mark 16:15–18). He says specifically, "In my name they will drive out demons" (v. 17).

We in the church today must be courageous enough to acknowledge our need to live in the reality of the nearness of the kingdom of God, for it is just as much at hand today as it was when Jesus first brought it to us two thousand years ago. I believe the primary purpose of the power of God given to believers is to be a continuing revelation of His love and an integral part of the presentation of the gospel[1]—which includes deliverance. How can someone embrace the good news of the gospel if they are bound by the powers of darkness?

God sent His Son to set the captives free, and Jesus is still releasing prisoners today. New Testament scholar Craig Keener, in his book *Miracles: The Credibility of the New Testament Accounts*, presents ample and credible evidence from his many years of research that both historical and modern day miracles, including deliverances, are genuine divine acts of a loving God. Gathering testimonies from all over the globe, he reports:

> Cameroonian Christians exorcised a person known to be insane; his immediate and full recovery led to many conversions in the community. Many Indian evangelists pray and fast, then minister to those who are held to be possessed; word of deliverances from spirits spreads, opening the community to the gospel. After Micronesian pastor Steve Malakai began

to rebuke the spiritual powers dominant in the ruins of an ancient sacrificial site, widespread healings, deliverances, and conversions followed. A Sri Lankan evangelist notes that he cast out demons, and converts turned over talismans and charms; people expected him to suffer harm, but he did not.[2]

Jesus is our conquering King! Notice that I did not say "was" our conquering King. Jesus *is* alive and active in the world today through His church to bring the words of the Lord's Prayer—"your kingdom come, your will be done, on earth as it is in heaven"[3]—to their fullness.

The faddish fascination with the devil and evil that enjoyed resurgence in American culture in the 1970s, and which teamed up with a yearning to broaden our consciousness, ushered in a plethora of occult-based New Age practices that have taken root in our culture. Combining that with the half-truths of the entertainment industry, we are left with a spiritually confused culture. Intellectual evangelicalism tends to strong-arm the notion of evil, and thus the need for deliverance; while other segments of the church race after deliverance to such a great extent, they see demons behind everything that ails them. Add to the mix people whose practice of deliverance borders on questionable and manipulative, and is it any wonder the church tends to throw up its hands in confusion when it comes to deliverance?

There is no need for the church to remain ignorant or confused about deliverance. If we examine the ministry of Jesus in its cultural context, we can more accurately assess our own cultural assumptions about healing. With their limited knowledge of medicine and science, the Gospel writers, especially Luke the physician, were able to distinguish between illness with a demonic root and illness with a physical root.

If Jesus's disciples were able to combine medical knowledge and spiritual insight and apply it to Jesus's ministry of healing, then perhaps we in the church today should be more willing to do the same in order to bring a holistic paradigm of healing to the body of Christ in the twenty-first century. After all, allopathic medicine has not proved to be the be-all and end-all of healing. What would a restoration of the New Testament reality of healing, including deliverance, look like for the church today? It would look like revival!

Having considered the New Testament's insights into demons and deliverance, we will now examine the church's historical understanding of them.

Chapter 4

DELIVERANCE IN THE HISTORY OF THE CHURCH

APOSTOLIC CHRISTIANITY WAS THE FOUNDATION of the early church, as its disciples went forth to evangelize and reconcile believers. The early church was composed largely of Jews who were protected to practice their faith under Roman law. With the destruction of Jerusalem and fledgling Christianity's instance of being the only "true" religion, persecution ensued. Add to this persecution Plato's dualistic philosophy that the spirit realm is superior to the natural realm, which ushered in the concept of the devaluation of the human body, and you find conditions coming together for the beginnings of the theological paradigm shift that would eventually lead to a cessation of the ministry of healing and deliverance within the church.

When I talk about the ministry of healing in the early church, understand that it encompassed deliverance.

Obviously not every healing necessitates deliverance, but deliverance in the early church was nonetheless an integral part of the ministry of healing. Quite often healing could not take place without deliverance, and that has not changed. The early church understood this. Morton Kelsey, in his book *Healing and Christianity*, examines reliable witnesses from early church history who witnessed and/or participated in healing and deliverance ministry. Justin Martyr is one such witness.

Justin Martyr was a Christian apologist in the second century who evangelized in Asia Minor and was eventually martyred in Rome for his faith. Before his death he wrote two "apologies" (a defense of a belief or position), one of which was addressed to the then emperor of Rome. Here is a quote from that apology, which indicates how the power of the finished work of Christ on the cross in the lives of the early disciples built the church:

> For numberless demoniacs throughout the whole world, and in your city, many of our Christian men exorcizing them in the Name of Jesus Christ…have healed and do heal, rendering helpless and driving the possessing devils out of the men, though they could not be cured by all the other exorcists, and those who used incantations and drugs.[1]

This strong emphasis on the ministry of healing and deliverance in the early church was foundational to the spread of Christianity and remains so today. The gospel is supernatural, and we cannot fully share its good news apart from the supernatural. The church must respond to the god of the age with faith *and* power.

EARLY EYEWITNESSES TO DELIVERANCE MINISTRY

There are a great many others throughout the history of the early church who bear witness to deliverance: Hermes (AD 150–270), Tertullian (AD 160–220), Origen (AD 185–254), Theophilus of Antioch, Marcus Minucius Felix (second century), Irenaeus (AD 175–195), and Arnobius and Lactantius (AD 300–325),[2] to name a few. Here is a testimony from Lactantius, who was a pupil of Arnobius:

> As He Himself before His passion put to confusion demons by His word and command, so now, by the name and sign of the same passion, unclean spirits, having insinuated themselves into the bodies of men, are driven out, when racked and tormented, and confessing themselves to be demons, they yield themselves to God, who harasses them.[3]

In AD 380 Christianity became the official religion of the Roman Empire. With this legitimacy, strong and brilliant leaders began to emerge within the church, forging the orthodoxy of the early Christian doctrines, of which healing and deliverance were an integral part. From this group emerged Augustine, who would become the undisputed theologian in the West for one thousand years.

Initially critical of healing, Augustine's experiences over a period of forty years led him to the reality that healing and deliverance were indeed an integral part of the work and ministry of the church. Before he died, Augustine would become known for a healing anointing and the authority to deliver.

In spite of this his theology, as it has been communicated within the Reformational churches, did not include his matured views on healing and deliverance. As a result, the reformers who followed Augustine abandoned the reality of evil in favor of a worldview that steered the church away from the biblical understanding of the supernaturally empowered church.

The disintegration of Western civilization with the collapse of the Roman Empire in the sixth and seventh centuries ushered in a new era for the church. As educational systems collapsed and cities emptied, disease, depression, and despair began to characterize life, moving the emphasis from "this life" to the next. With the translation of the Scriptures into Latin, the meaning of some parts of Scripture was inadvertently mistranslated. The word *heal* was sometimes translated as "save." With the change in meaning came a change in practice. In the Catholic church, the anointing to heal became known as the "Extreme Unction for Dying."

The church's rise to power and the affluence that resulted led to a decline in the morality of church leaders and gave rise to the monastic movement— which actually comprised a series of movements that resembled holiness revivals. The monastics, pursuing a level of holiness that no longer existed in the church, fled the cities seeking refuge in the deserts of North Africa where they continued to practice healing and deliverance. They eventually became known as the "Desert Fathers." In the midst of doctrinal battles the *charismata* lost its place as a vital part of the institutional church.

Eddie L. Hyatt, in his book *2000 Years of Charismatic Christianity*,[4] says this:

> Following Constantine's ascent to power, most supernatural phenomena are recorded either by monastics or by those who venerated the

monastic lifestyle. Cardinal Leon Joseph Suenens is correct in saying, "In its beginnings, monasticism was, in fact, a Charismatic movement."[5] The miraculous gifts of the Holy Spirit, which disappeared from the institutional church, now appeared among the monastics. Many monks gained notoriety for their power in prayer and their ability to produce healing, deliverance from demonic oppression and other miraculous phenomena.

One such monk was Antony, considered the founder of monasticism.[6] The son of an affluent Christian family in Egypt, he answered a call from God at age eighteen to enter the monastic lifestyle. Bishop Athanasius wrote a biography of Antony, which is "filled with accounts of the supernatural. According to Athanasius, many people from all walks of life visited Antony in the desert seeking his prayers and wisdom. He is said to have possessed the gift of discerning of spirits and often knew things supernaturally. His prayers brought healing to the sick and deliverance to the demonized... Many gathered at the entrance of Antony's cave seeking his prayers... and 'through him the Lord healed the bodily ailments of many present, and cleansed others from evil spirits.'"[7]

The church came to believe that these divine Desert Fathers were among the few holy enough to practice healing and deliverance. Priests and nuns were also included in this "holy enough" category. So-called normal believers who continued to move in those gifts were suspected of operating by the power of the devil.

THE INFLUENCE OF GREEK PHILOSOPHIES

In the thirteenth century the increasing influence of Greek philosophies began to lead the church away from the first-century paradigm of healing. During the period 1200–1575 the church came under the influence of a theology called the Aquinas-Aristotelian Synthesis. Thomas Aquinas was an Italian Dominican theologian considered one of the most influential theologians of the medieval period. His ideas on integrating Christian thought and Aristotelian philosophy had a significant impact during a critical juncture of Western culture. It is important to note that his ideas took quite a long time to make a significant impact. It was a gradual process, rather than a sudden event. Nevertheless, the more rational approach to the doctrine of the church made experience less important.

Augustine (AD 354–430), bishop of Hippo in North Africa, initially dismissed the *charismata* as signs that had passed away from the church, stating that "the Holy

Spirit's presence is no longer given by miracles, but by the love of God in one's heart for the church."[8] Later in his life Augustine came to understand the supernatural at work in the life of the church and wrote about it in his work *The City of God* describing, in addition to a variety of specific healings, "demon possession and even the raising of the dead."[9]

The Reformers of the 1500s, who failed to understand that power flows out of relationship and not doctrine, embraced a theology that opposed healing and deliverance. Fortunately the advancement of the kingdom of God has never been subject to the theology of man. God continues to demonstrate His power to those who are humble enough to receive it.

The rise of Protestantism and its accompanying theology clashed sharply with the theology of the Catholic Church, creating a great divide in the Christian world. Martin Luther led the charge away from Catholicism. Many came to characterize Luther as anti-miraculous, but that was not the case. "Luther left clear evidence of his own belief in the personal and direct ministry of the Spirit... Luther is often quoted as saying, 'Often has it happened, and still does, that devils have been driven out in the name of Christ; also by calling on His name and prayer, the sick have been healed.'"[10]

DELIVERANCE REBOUNDS WITH
GREAT AWAKENINGS

The revival movements of the eighteenth and nine-teenth centuries centered on a desire for holiness and a return to apostolic Christianity. These mighty moves of God, commonly known as the First and Second Great Awakening, saw hundreds of thousands of churches planted worldwide, new denominations birthed, and the gifts of the Spirit restored. Healing and deliverance once again became major reasons, like they were in the Book of Acts, that people came to Christ.

Stories of deliverance abound from those two centu-ries of revival. One of the first occurred in Germany in the 1800s at the beginning of what was known as the Faith Cure movement. A Lutheran pastor and theolo-gian named Johann Blumhardt undertook to deliver a young woman in his parish. From the fall of 1841 until 1842 the entire village and surrounding area where the young woman lived witnessed Blumhardt's very public battle with the demonic. When the demon finally left her, it shouted, "Jesus is victor!" on its way out. Heard over a mile away, the shout brought a change in the spiritual atmosphere of the region, resulting in a spir-itual awakening as people streamed to Blumhardt to tearfully confess their sins and receive prayers for healing. By Easter the community was experiencing a powerful move of God's Spirit.

Brothers John and Charles Wesley, dubbed "the head and the heart of revival," were eighteenth-century British Anglican clerics who, along with George Whitefield, founded Methodism. Historian Roberts Liardon, in his book *God's General's*, details the story of the deliverance of a man named John Hayden.

Hayden, an upstanding man well known in his community, attended one of Wesley's meetings only to come away denouncing Wesley's teaching as delusion. When he sat down later to read one of Wesley's sermons titled "Salvation by Faith," the conviction of God came upon him with such power that his wife found him thrashing on the floor and crying out, "Let all the world see the judgment of God!"[11]

Hayden then began to renounce the demons that were tormenting him, telling them: "Thou canst not stay. Christ will cast thee out!"[12] John Wesley and his brother were called to Hayden's home where they proceeded to pray until he had been delivered.

In another account, from one of the Wesleys' prayer meetings in October 1739, a young woman was dramatically delivered. As John was preaching, she fell to the ground, gnashing her teeth and roaring. With great difficulty, three or four people were able to hold her down so that her violent symptoms could subside. Interspersed with periods of calm, she would begin screaming and spitting and spewing blasphemy. At times she would be overcome with hideous laughter. At other times the demons would speak. This went on for the better part of the afternoon before the woman was delivered.[13]

Rejected by the church, Wesley was forced into itinerant ministry in the English countryside. There "the Spirit confirmed the Word with healings, with deliverances and with unusual manifestations such as falling, trembling, roaring, crying and laughing."[14]

The ministry of Charles Finney, considered the father of modern revivalism, touched the fabric of America at the juncture of war in the early 1800s. It is said that "the power of the Holy Spirit worked mightily in him to transform the emerging culture of New England from impotent Calvinism into active and effective evangelism wherever he went."[15]

Finney was an anointed evangelist. His innovative teaching inspired a fledgling country to become one nation under God. In his sermon titled "The Christian Warfare," published in 1843, Finney says, "The Christian warfare is a war between the will and Satan. It is his great object to keep the will in subjection to the propensities of the sensibility. Hence he directs all his efforts to arouse these propensities, and through them to enslave the will."[16]

In his sermon Finney relates the story of a man who experienced deliverance during one of his (Finney's) meetings. This very ungodly man, who took great delight in heaping verbal abuse upon Christianity just for sport, came to Finney's meeting with the express purpose of being disruptive. As Finney preached, the power of God came upon this man. He fell from his seat to the floor where he proceeded to writhe in great agony, crying out, "Oh, Jesus, how I have abused Thee!" This continued until finally the man fell silent and peaceful. He went on to become what Finney termed "a flaming light" for Christ whose "tongue seems to be tuned with the praises of God."[17]

Estimates are that Finney led more than five hundred thousand people to salvation. At times huge crowds responded to the presence of God in Finney's meetings with repentance. When he came to town, bars closed for lack of patrons, businesses were shuttered so employees could avail themselves of the man of God, and crime dropped off. Like everyone involved in the mighty moves of God, Finney had his critics. Certainly not everyone in the church embraced this extended period of revival. Some seventy years later British preacher, evangelist, and Bible scholar George Campbell Morgan, for example, viewed the revival movements this way: "Pentecostalism is the last vomit of Satan."

DELIVERANCE MAKES NEWS IN THE TWENTIETH CENTURY

A mid-twentieth-century story of deliverance comes from the ministry of US pastor Lester Sumrall. He and his family were called to ministry in Manila in the 1950s. It was there that Sumrall's work with a demon-possessed girl drew national attention. Her story, titled "Bitten by Demons," is detailed in the first chapter of his book *Demons: The Answer Book*.[18] This young woman, a jail inmate, was repeatedly bitten, although no one could see anything biting her. Bites appeared on her knee, neck, arms, and shoulders. Teeth marks could be seen, wet with saliva.

As she was being bitten she would scream and thrash about trying to fight off her attackers even as she was held in the arms of her jailers. She described one of the demons who bit her as having dark curly hair on its body, large sharp eyes and fangs.

At one point her anguished battle with the devil was broadcast over the city radio station. Sumrall heard the broadcast and recognized immediately that the girl was not mad or sick, but demon possessed.

He cried out to God for direction and felt God telling him to go to the jail and pray for her, and God would deliver her.

In obedience Sumrall went to the prison and was granted permission to minister to the girl. As he began to minister, a battle ensued between the devil and Sumrall. It raged throughout the day. That evening, exhausted, Sumrall went home to rest, fast, and pray. He returned the next day and commenced to battle again on the girl's behalf. Eventually the demons were driven out of the girl, and she was set free.

So dramatic and public were her deliverance and healing that newspapers carried the story all over the Philippines. The entire country became open to the gospel as a result of this girl's deliverance. Revival meetings sprang up and continued for weeks with crowds estimated to have reached sixty thousand in one night. It was reported that one hundred and fifty thousand were saved over the course of the revival. Healings abounded. "A famous actor who couldn't walk was healed...A lawyer who'd been on crutches for twelve years walked out holding them in his arms totally healed."[19]

While the early church had a rich history of healing with deliverance, and certain segments of the church today do also, by and large most non-Pentecostal/charismatic Christians have little interest in healing and deliverance within Christianity. It is only when someone, be they clergy or laity, has a direct personal experience with the demonic—like the three seminarians I mentioned in my introduction—that they become open to the ministry of deliverance. The good news in all of this is that with the rise of occult practices in Western society, we are beginning to see, out of necessity, cracks in the walls of resistance surrounding deliverance ministry.

Having first looked at the impact of my personal experience upon my understanding of deliverance, followed by a study of the Old and New Testaments' perspectives on demons and deliverance and a consideration of the church's perspective, let us now turn our attention to what I believe is the purpose of the ministry of deliverance.

I believe the ministry of deliverance must be understood as part of the "sanctification process." This is the subject of our next three chapters. We will begin in chapter 5 by addressing the question of whether or not a Christian can have a demon, and then in chapter 6 we will examine the signs of demonization. With this foundation, we will examine deliverance as part of the process of sanctification in chapter 7.

Chapter 5

CAN A CHRISTIAN BE DEMONIZED?

❖━━━◆◆◆◆◆━━━❖

A NUMBER OF YEARS AGO I WAS MINISTERING with a team in India. We were praying for the healing of a young man who had suffered from migraine headaches for ten years. He was about twenty-five years old and had experienced a migraine every waking moment of his life for the previous ten years. A few nights earlier he had seen half the crowd of about one hundred thousand people healed and about a third of them accept Jesus. Most were Hindus. This young man was a Muslim and asked if our God would do for him what He had done for the Hindus. I told him I believed that God would heal him as well, and we began to pray for him. The moment we began to pray for his healing, his eyes rolled back in his head so that you couldn't see anything but the whites. He began to scream—a high-pitched scream like a woman's—and to stick his tongue out in a bizarre way. Then he fell over.

I told our translator he had a demon and that we needed to get it out. We did, and afterward the young man came to me, excited that for the first time in ten years his headache was gone. That was wonderful news, but I knew we had another problem, and I told him so. I explained to him it was a spirit (demon) that had caused his headaches and we had cast it out in Jesus's name; but if he didn't have Jesus inside him, then the afflicting spirit and the headaches would return. If he did not belong to Jesus, then he did not have the authority to use the name of Jesus. In other words, he could remain a Muslim and see the return of the migraines or become a Christian and have the authority to stay free. With no argument on his behalf, he asked what he needed to do to accept Jesus, and one of the pastors led him to the Lord. Outside of Christ, this young man had nothing with which to deal with the demonic. And that is true for everyone.

If someone is not a believer and wishes to receive deliverance, we can lead them to the Lord before we minister deliverance, or we can expel the demon and then lead them to Christ immediately afterward. Either way works.

Over the years many people have asked me if a Christian can be demonized. The most demonized person in the Bible, and the classic example of deliverance, is found in Mark 5. It's the story of the madman of Gadara, and it is this account that leads me to believe that Christians can be demonized.

WHAT DOES IT MEAN TO BE "DEMONIZED"?

Before we go any further, I want to examine the word *demonized* as it is used in this book. Most English translations of the Bible use either the term *possession* or "those possessed." I consider that a poor choice of words because it is not found in the Greek. It makes no distinction between *possess*, *obsess*, and *oppressed*. It is just one word with a diversity of meanings, and a form of the word for *demon*. It is through transliteration that we get the word *demonized*.

Let's use a CD as an illustration. A CD works by laser light. Most of the time CDs work just fine; they play perfectly. But when a gouge or a scratch damages a CD, the laser light hangs up when it hits that damaged spot. This is a metaphor for a little bit of demonization. When a person has a "little bit of demonization" everything in life works fine, but there is this one spot, a hang-up, that pushes your button, and when the light hits that spot, the problem is revealed.

On the other hand, you might have a CD that has been badly treated and has all types of fingerprints, gunk, and scratches on it. When you try to play it, sometimes it works, sometimes it doesn't. It hangs up a lot. That is also a metaphor for *demonized*. The same word is used for both situations, but one is more severe than the other.

A third metaphor is a CD left on the backseat of the car in the hot sun of summer. It warps and won't even go into the CD player. It doesn't work at all. This is a metaphor for the most severe scenario—in which a person's life has been so impaired by the demonic they are not able to function in a healthy way. In Greek the same word is used for all three categories, but in English we try to use several words: *possessed*, *oppressed*, *obsessed*. We have tried to change the meaning of the Greek. John Wimber believed that it is better to use the one word, *demonized*, with the understanding that it can mean from mild to severe.

CHRISTIANS AND DEMONIZATION

Now I do not believe that a Christian can be totally demonized. And I do not believe that a Christian can be possessed. The Bible says that we have been bought with a price, the precious blood of Jesus Christ. We are *His* possession, therefore we can never become the possession of the enemy, nor can we be totally possessed by the enemy if we are born again. That being said, I do not believe a Christian can be possessed according to what is usually understood by the term *possessed*.

However, I do believe a Christian can be demonized or influenced by evil spirits. Wimber said it this way: he did not believe a demon could have, or "own," a Christian because he didn't believe a demon could possess a Christian. If we are born again we belong to Christ, therefore a demon cannot own us or possess us. So, even though a demon cannot have a Christian, a Christian can have a demon.

Think with me for a moment. The argument is, if the Holy Spirit is in you, then how could there be an evil spirit in you? Let's follow this argument to its logical conclusion.

What are the *omni* definitions for God? *Omnipotence* is one: to be "all powerful." *Omniscience* is another: "all knowing." But what is the other one? It is *omnipresent*, which means that there is nowhere in the world where God's Spirit is not present. God is present everywhere. By that definition, an evil presence cannot be in the presence of God, so logically we would have to conclude that the devil and demons cannot be anywhere in the world because God is everywhere. And if they cannot exist where He is, then they cannot exist. It is easy to see that this kind of logic can lead one to dismiss evil. I don't believe that logic, but there are those who do.

The argument has also been made that if we are full of the Holy Spirit then we can't have a demon in us. I agree with that. I just don't believe that most Christians are *full* of the Holy Spirit—or remain full at all times. We can be full of the Holy Spirit and have something happen to us that causes us to respond in an unbiblical way. When we do that, we set ourselves up, creating an opening for affliction. We need to develop the spiritual habit of a biblical response to the trials of life so that the enemy cannot find any opening through which he can bring affliction.

It's important to understand, though, that not all instances of demonic affliction are the result of our unbiblical response to situations in life. Quite often demonic affliction comes through generational sin. The sins of the parents can be passed down to the children who are not yet able to understand or develop spiritual muscles to protect themselves. For this reason, ministering deliverance to children should be undertaken only with great caution and a full understanding of the dynamics of the situation.

Many people in America do not believe children can become demonized. We must remember that the forces of evil do not play by the rules of the Geneva Convention, the treaties that address the treatment of civilians, prisoners of war, and others affected by war worldwide.

There are no civilians in this war for souls, and women and children are special targets. I have seen small children demonized. Twice in the Bible we see children who are demonized, both instances in the Gospel of Mark. In Mark 9:14–29 Jesus heals a demonized boy. When He questions the boy's father about how long his son has been afflicted, He is told that it has been from childhood. In Mark 7:24–30 we see Jesus healing a girl who has been afflicted by a demon.

DELIVERANCE AND GOD'S COVENANT

Both believers and unbelievers alike can be demonically afflicted, but the Bible tells us specifically *who* the ministry of deliverance is intended for. All *can* be delivered, but not all *are* to be delivered, and understanding this distinction is very important when ministering deliverance.

In Luke 13:10–17 we see Jesus healing a woman who had been disabled by a demon for eighteen years, causing her to be bent over at all times. Jesus calls this woman "a daughter of Abraham"—meaning, a child of God in covenant relationship with God—and declares that she "should" be set free from Satan's afflicting grip. The fact that she is in a covenant relationship means that deliverance is available to her.

The story about the girl who was healed in Mark 7:24–30 gives us a fuller picture of who is eligible for deliverance. Her mother was a Syrophoenician, which meant she was a Gentile, not a Jew. Under the old covenant Jews were the people who were eligible to be delivered from evil spirits. Under the new covenant you must be a believer to be delivered—or become a believer so as not to be demonized again. Jesus came first for the house of Israel, the Jews. It was only after His resurrection that the Gentiles were included in the benefits of His atoning death.

It was at that point that the Gentiles were grafted into Israel and became covenant people. Before Jesus's death the children of Abraham were God's covenant people under the Old Covenant. The finished work of Christ on the cross ushered in the new covenant, opening up God's saving grace to Jew and Gentile alike.

When the Syrophoenician woman asked Jesus to heal her daughter, His response was that it is not right to take the children's bread and give it to the dogs. To the first-century Jews, *dog* was a euphemism for Gentiles. As harsh as His statement sounds to us, Jesus was telling her that the time had not yet come for His ministry to be available to the Gentiles. In other words, her daughter was not eligible for deliverance. The woman heard Jesus's explanation but was undeterred in pressing Him for her daughter's healing. She told Him that as a "dog" (Gentile), she was so desperate to see her daughter healed that she would take the crumbs that fell from His table. She was saying that she wasn't expecting her position as a Gentile to change yet; rather she was willing to receive the future healing that would be available for her daughter if Jesus would give it to her at that moment. She was a woman of great faith, and Jesus saw this. He healed her daughter as a result of her faith.

When Jesus spoke to this woman about "the children's bread," He was using a metaphor for Himself. Jesus is the bread of life, and the "children" are the children of God, those in covenant relationship with Him. What Jesus was saying is that the ministry of deliverance is not for the lost—those outside a covenant relationship with God. They can receive deliverance, but it is not intended for them because it will not hold. When He speaks of the children's bread, He is talking about deliverance and healing. We see in the Gospels, particularly in the books of Luke and Matthew, that deliverance was part of the ministry of healing.

If someone is not in covenant relationship with God, then it would be foolish to deliver them because the empty "space" occupied by the ousted demon would be vulnerable to the return of the demonic. The Holy Spirit would not be present to fill the unattended space. When demons see an open, unattended place, they return in force, and the person will be visited with an affliction greater than the one they experienced before they were delivered.[1]

The early church understood that deliverance is for the Christian but not the unbeliever. If you go back to the oldest liturgies of baptism, to the second century—when baptisms in the Catholic Church still were by immersion—you find that adults, mainly, were the ones being baptized.

The prayer of deliverance was not prayed before the baptism but after the person had come up from the baptismal waters. It was done this way because they believed baptism brought them life in Christ and put them in right relationship with Him. The overwhelming majority of adults being baptized in the church at that time were coming out of paganism. As they came up out of the baptismal waters, they experienced their moment of conversion, surrendering their commitment to paganism. So it was at that point any prayers for deliverance were ministered and they were filled with the Holy Spirit, not before.

Reasoning and philosophy led the church down the path of rejecting the belief that deliverance should be for the believer but not the unbeliever. That, in turn, led to thinking that if God is in you, then you cannot have a demon in you as well.

Let's turn our attention now to the signs of demonization.

Chapter 6

SIGNS OF DEMONIZATION

———— ❖ ————

I AM OFTEN ASKED, "HOW DO YOU KNOW YOU ARE dealing with a demon?" I believe the gift of discerning of spirits enables us to recognize the difference between natural and demonic physical and mental afflictions.

During the late 1980s I planted a new church in the southern suburbs of St. Louis, Missouri. We began with small groups called Kinships that met in people's homes. In these gatherings people would worship, give words of knowledge, prophesy, pray for healing, and study the Bible. One night a woman I will call "Mary" came to a Kinship group. Mary was Catholic. I had met her through our volunteer work at a local food bank called Feed My People.

Mary had a problem with pain in her shoulder and asked for healing prayer. As we began to interview her to determine the source of the problem, and thereby how to pray more specifically, we learned the pain would wake her up several times during the night, making it impossible for her to get a good night's rest. There didn't seem to be a natural cause for the pain, such as an accident or an injury to the shoulder. Neither did arthritis run in her family. There had been no altercations that might have resulted in some type of curse being involved. And she had not been involved in New Age or spiritualist meetings that would have opened her up to being demonized. Unsure of the cause of her pain, we began to pray, speaking healing to her shoulder.

When a curse is spoken over someone, the result can be anything from a relatively mild affliction, such as Mary's pain in her shoulder, to severe physical or mental affliction such as was experienced by a woman I ministered to in Brazil. She experienced severe physical deformity as a result of a curse. Her story is detailed in chapter 8 when we take a more in-depth look at curses.

AFFLICTING SPIRITS

When we first began to pray for Mary, she was not in pain, but as I prayed, the pain began. This can be one sign that a physical problem has a spiritual root—that is, an afflicting spirit. After a brief time of prayer I stopped to reinterview her and find out what was happening. She told us the pain was gone from her left shoulder but that it had instantly moved to her neck. If pain starts moving around in someone's body when they are being prayed for, it is a sign that an afflicting spirit is at work. Knowing this, I changed the way I was praying and began to address the afflicting spirit, commanding it to leave in Jesus's name. She then said, "The pain has left my neck and now is in my right shoulder." Again I said, "I command this spirit of affliction to leave Mary's shoulder in Jesus's name. Get out!" Mary responded, "The pain is gone." But a few seconds later she added, "It is now in my elbow."

I continued to command the spirit of affliction to leave in Jesus's name. It left her elbow and went into her wrist. As I commanded the spirit again to leave in Jesus's name, it went from her wrist into her fingers. I again commanded it to leave in the name of Jesus. It left her fingers and must have exited her body altogether because she announced that she was pain free. When I saw her again a few weeks later she told me, "I haven't had any pain or been awakened during the night with pain since you prayed for me." Over a decade later she remained free of the pain that had been so devastating to her.

You often may hear the term *afflicting spirit* used in deliverance ministry. It is just another word for *demon*. Afflicting spirits that affect us psychologically can do so only when they have been given authority to, through an open door. They can impact the way we think and feel and can twist our emotions so that we behave in aberrant and ungodly ways.

When an afflicting spirit attacks the body rather than the realm of the soul, it does not need the authority of an open door. It can simply attack, such as the one did in Mary's case. In the case of the woman in the Bible who was bent over by an evil spirit,[1] there was apparently no root cause that brought on her affliction. We see Jesus simply commanding the afflicting spirit to leave her.

I remember the time I experienced two of the greatest miracles of my ministry. At the very moment they happened, at home thousands of miles away, my one-year-old son, Jeremiah, became the victim of collateral damage from an afflicting spirit. He awoke from a sound sleep, screaming from the pain of a severe earache he did not have when he went to bed. My wife, DeAnne, sat with him and prayed for him but couldn't get him to stop screaming unless she prayed in tongues. DeAnne had to sit with him, praying in tongues until 5:00 a.m. before the attack subsided. I believe an afflicting spirit attacked him as a result of the miracles that were taking place as I ministered. It was the only earache he ever had, and now he is twenty-two.

Afflicting spirits will try to return, and can return, to the person from whom they have been cast out. We need to remember to counsel people we have ministered to, equipping them with the knowledge that they have the authority to command any afflicting spirit to leave if it tries to return. These spirits can be very persistent, and sometimes a person will have to be even more persistent to get the spirit to give up and go away. If a person does not understand their authority, an afflicting spirit can convince them they are not healed. When this happens, authority has been yielded and the demon can return along with the affliction.

PHYSICAL MANIFESTATIONS

Although not all physical and mental afflictions are demonic, certain physical manifestations can indicate demonization, such as the pain that manifested in Mary's body. You may also see sudden drowsiness, facial contortions, screaming, a rigid body, a lack of eye contact, or eyes that roll around, especially rolling back so you can only see the whites of the eyes, and changing voices. Remember, demons do not always manifest, and physical manifestations such as these do not always indicate the presence of a demon. Each instance needs to be investigated and evaluated to determine the root cause. The Holy Spirit is always available to guide us with discernment.

As we evaluate the situations that come before us in the course of deliverance ministry, it is important to keep in mind that the devil seeks to humiliate the people of God and will miss no opportunity to do so. By studying the accounts of demonization in the Bible we can better understand the ways that Satan chooses to humiliate people. In the Gospels the demonized are described as naked, removed from society and isolated, chained, filthy, and engaging in humiliating and destructive behaviors such as throwing themselves on the ground or into a fire, shrieking and ranting, and exhibiting a superhuman strength that makes them uncontrollable and dangerous.

In the story of the Gerasene demoniac in Mark 5 we see clearly some of the signs of demonization, which I will discuss in a moment. But as you read the account that follows, I think it is very important to note that even the most demonized person in the Bible still had the freedom to come to Jesus. The enemy could not keep him away from the Lord:

> They went across the lake to the region of the Gerasenes. When Jesus got out of the boat, a man with an impure spirit came from the tombs to

meet him. This man lived in the tombs, and no one could bind him anymore, not even with a chain. For he had often been chained hand and foot, but he tore the chains apart and broke the irons on his feet. No one was strong enough to subdue him. Night and day among the tombs and in the hills he would cry out and cut himself with stones. When he saw Jesus from a distance, he ran and fell on his knees in front of him. He shouted at the top of his voice, "What do you want with me, Jesus, Son of the Most High God? In God's name don't torture me!" For Jesus had said to him, "Come out of this man, you impure spirit!" Then Jesus asked him, "What is your name?" "My name is Legion," he replied, "for we are many." And he begged Jesus again and again not to send them out of the area. A large herd of pigs was feeding on the nearby hillside. The demons begged Jesus, "Send us among the pigs; allow us to go into them." He gave them permission, and the impure spirits came out and went into the pigs. The herd, about two thousand in number, rushed down the steep bank into the lake and were drowned. Those tending the pigs ran off and reported this in the town and countryside, and the people went out to see what had happened. When they came to Jesus, they saw the man who had been possessed by the legion of demons, sitting there, dressed and in his right mind; and they were afraid. Those who had seen it told the people what had happened to the demon-possessed man—and told about the pigs as well. Then the people began to plead with Jesus to leave their region. As Jesus was getting into the boat, the man who had been demon-possessed begged to go with him. Jesus did not let him, but said, "Go home to your own people and tell them how much the Lord has done for you, and how he has had mercy on you." So the man went away and began to tell in the Decapolis how much Jesus had done for him. And all the people were amazed.

—MARK 5:1–20

SIGNS OF DEMONIZATION: WHAT TO LOOK FOR

Here, then, are the key signs that indicate a person is being demonized. Remember, each instance you encounter should be evaluated; the Holy Spirit is there to guide you with discernment.

1. Isolation, particularly from family.

2. Out-of-control behavior.

3. Doing things intentionally to hurt oneself, including self-mutilation such as cutting.

4. Humiliation. The demonic likes to humiliate both the person and their family.

5. Mental illness. Mental illness can be a sign of demonic oppression or demonization, but it is important to understand that not all or even most mental illness is necessarily demonic in origin.

Isolation. At the top of the list is isolation and separation, particularly from family. The man Jesus encountered was not living at home anymore. He was living amid the tombs, in a place of death. We can guess that his behavior had become so damaging and dangerous to his family that he was forced to leave. Or perhaps he left on his own. It does not say, but the point is that regardless of why, a separation had occurred between the demonized man and his family. His behavior, and the shame and guilt it brought, caused a separation. When we see this happening in someone's life, it is a sign that something evil is in operation. It is very common to see this with alcoholism, drug addiction, violent temper that can't be controlled, and sexual perversion.

Out-of-control behavior. Even though he was chained, the man possessed a supernatural strength that enabled him to break free. He was physically out

65

of control in a dangerous way. The petite young woman receiving counseling from two of my seminary professors I mentioned earlier exhibited this same sort of supernatural strength.

There is also the type of out-of-control behavior that causes a person to do things they do not want to do. Overwhelmingly strong motivational drives, in the form of temptations and compulsions, can grip a person. Often we will hear someone who is caught in addictive and compulsive behavior say they do not want to engage in the behavior but are powerless to stop, even to the point of self-hatred. Both of these types of out-of-control behaviors can be signs of demonization.

Harm to self. The third sign of demonization is inflicting harm to oneself—doing things intentionally to hurt oneself, including forms of self-mutilation, such as cutting. The Scripture tells us the man would cry out and cut himself with stones.

I remember the first cutter I ever met. She was from a wealthy family in the area. Her father was a top executive with a large company—a mover and shaker. She lived in a very affluent area and would drive about thirty minutes to attend one of our Kinship groups. She was bipolar and a cutter, with a very poor self-image. She told me I could never come to her house.

One day, I don't know why, I felt that I was supposed to go to her home. I arrived and rang the doorbell. She was there, and even though she did not want to invite me in, she was polite enough to let me inside.

As soon as I stepped through the door, I realized why she didn't want me there. I am not normally a *feeler*, someone who easily senses or discerns the spiritual environment around them, but I could feel the oppression when I walked into her house. It was very strong.

The house was in disarray. It was daytime, but all the blinds were pulled. The house was dark, and there was a look of oppression everywhere. Things were disheveled. It was a very fine home but very messy. There were stacks of stuff as far as the eye could see. I saw a wealth of books on witchcraft and the occult. I came to find out that her mother was into the occult.

When a person engages in occult activities, they open not only themselves to evil but also their children. It is likely in this woman's case that both her bipolar issues and the cutting were rooted in the dark spirituality taking place in the home because of her mother's occult activities.

Humiliation. The demonic loves to humiliate people and their families. The fact that demons like to humiliate the person is why Bottari teaches that we must not let a demon cause a person to throw up or to manifest in other humiliating ways. Although many people operate under the assumption that a person must manifest in the midst of deliverance in order to be delivered, this is not the case. If a demon begins to manifest, we are to order them to stop and then advise the person that they do not need to yield to the demonic. Demons should never be allowed the upper hand in deliverance ministry.

Mental illness. This is the fifth and final sign on our list. As I have stated before, not all mental illness has a demonic root; it can be, however, a sign of demonic oppression, demonization, or mental problems. It often can manifest in humiliating behavior.

The first person I prayed for who was healed of mental illness was a man in my church. He had been married before, but mental illness had cost him his wife and children. His disorder caused him to have total breaks with reality. Every year, even though he was on medication, he would have episodes that would send him to the hospital for up to two weeks. One time he stripped naked and ran through the streets. Another time he stood up in a meeting and called a leading evangelist a false prophet and said a lot of horrible things. His behavior was terribly humiliating to himself and to his family.

He was engaged when I ministered to him but was worried that his mental illness would doom his second attempt at family life. The first time we met for prayer, I sat him down, put my hand on his head, blessed him, and then prayed for him. I think I prayed for a good half hour or longer. At one point he told me that he felt something going on inside his head. God healed this dear man, and he went on to live a normal life. He was never hospitalized again. He remarried, had children, became a leader in my church, and was promoted to assistant manager at his job.

DEMONIC HUMILIATION

When I was twenty-one, I took the pastorate of a small church in a little rural village. The denomination was quite liberal, but the church itself was conservative. My first Sunday I realized the Sunday school consisted of about six women all over sixty, and the worship attendance was twelve. This little village was like a slum, and the presence of the demonic was noticeable.

The house next to the parsonage was blackboard without any siding on it, with a car on blocks in the yard and an engine sitting on the front porch. The woman who lived there was mentally ill. I came to learn that she had run several pastors out of town. She had once been pretty, but now she was rather heavy and no longer attractive and wore garish lipstick painted on her face way above her mouth.

From time to time she would run over and knock on the door of the parsonage. Not knowing it was her, I would open the door, and there she was. She would turn around and ask to be zipped up. It was a bad situation. She had been an annoyance to several pastors in that small community.

Just down the block was a family in which the daughters, ages twelve and thirteen, would climb onto the roof of the house to keep their father from raping them. And on the edge of town was a nice house where a young family lived who had two or three children in grade school. When the bus would pull up to pick up the children, the mother would sometimes come outside wearing only her panties and bra.

All of this humiliating behavior was heartbreaking. The enemy comes to kill, steal, and destroy,[2] and demonic humiliation accomplishes all of those things when it manifests in the life of a person and their family. Humiliation has great power in the spirit realm—it brings death, not life. Humiliation is not of God. When you see humiliating situations occurring, there is a very good chance that a demonic spirit is at work.

In Mark 5:15 it says, "When they came to Jesus, they saw the man *who had been* possessed by the legion of demons, sitting there, dressed and in his right mind" (emphasis added). The spirit of humiliation had been broken—the man now was clothed and in his right mind.

MISINTERPRETING THE SIGNS

Over the years I have had discussions about deliverance with Dr. Pablo Deiros, president of International Baptist Theological Seminary in Buenos Aires, Argentina. I consider him one of the most brilliant religious scholars in the world today.

From his years of involvement with deliverance ministry in South America and across the world, Dr. Deiros has observed that most people in the North American church do not believe the Western church has demons. We tend to think of deliverance issues as belonging in South American and African cultures, but not in our Western culture. According to Dr. Deiros, however, America is one of the most demonized cultures he has ever encountered.

Rather than acknowledging the demonic, we in the West tend to attach psychological or medical terminology to situations that really are demonic. Too often we cover up the demonic with mental-illness categories. Again I am not saying that *all* or even most mental illness is rooted in the demonic. And I am not saying that no one in the church of North America acknowledges the demonic.

What I am saying is that deliverance is often misunderstood in the North American church today—or dismissed entirely. Our seminaries need to be equipped to train pastors to understand deliverance, to know how to minister it, and to know how to train others to minister it. While there are many fine ministries that train in deliverance, unless this type of training is offered at the seminary level, the majority of pastors will not receive it.

DEMONIZATION AND THE SUBCONSCIOUS

Many behaviors we encounter in deliverance ministry are subconscious. Sometimes we behave in certain ways due to inner hurts and wounds, unaware that we are being driven subconsciously. The enemy takes advantage of our subconscious pain and comes in, using these hurts to manipulate us, while often bringing deception or accusation that causes us to do things we normally wouldn't. When someone tells us they feel compulsively driven to do things and they don't know why, we know there is usually a hurt with something demonic riding on top of it. That is when the inner-healing connection with deliverance fits in so powerfully.

I myself have experienced deliverance and inner healing. There was a time when I was very critical of myself, very judgmental of my failures and temptations. Even though I was not yielding to temptation, the fact that I was tempted bothered me. During the process of inner healing I learned that some of the issues I struggled with throughout my life were not just bad choices, but also deep needs in my subconscious that were rooted in rejection. The rejection had caused me to behave in certain ways; yet I had no understanding of the root cause of my behavior.

I do not mean to imply that I was not responsible for my behavior; I was responsible. But I came to understand that my will was not as free as I liked to think. I was bound by subconscious needs born of rejection. These were deep, powerful wounds and hurts that went back to before I was born and of which I had no cognitive understanding. These wounds exerted a powerful impact on the way I felt about myself. They became like inner buttons that could be pushed easily when I felt hurt or rejected. When they were pushed, I reacted in ways that often were unbecoming. As I progressed through inner healing and came to understand the dynamics of my own woundedness, I was able to forgive myself.

Two Misguided Views of Demonization

When it comes to dealing with the demonic we must be careful not to think that (1) everything is demonic or (2) nothing is demonic. Both mind-sets are equally misguided. We must exercise spiritual discernment and understand what the Bible has to say.

One way we can try to determine the presence of demons is by asking probing questions. But we should always be mindful that the person we are dealing with must be given priority. Deliverance is an act of love. We do not want to sacrifice a person by laying them on the altar of an agenda of deliverance that could possibly scar them or wound them. Our priority is always the healing of the person, done in an atmosphere of honor and love.

Certainly not all physical illness is rooted in the demonic. Our bodies can malfunction due to physical issues. The same is true of mental illness. Not all mental illness has a demonic root. The brain is an organ that can malfunction just like any other organ in the body. A malfunctioning body or brain may be caused by a physical/chemical issue or a spiritual issue or both.

Abuse, for example, can impact brain function. If someone was abused as a child, they may have developed patterns of disassociation. This puts their brain in survival mode by partitioning off parts of it so the person can disassociate with other parts. This protective mechanism enables the person to survive as a child, but if left unresolved, can cause dysfunction in adulthood, leading to a fragmented personality. This is a survival mechanism of the mind, not a demon. Demons can attach to these disassociated parts of the mind and can even masquerade as a disassociated personality, but casting out those demons will not heal the person. They will be healed when their inner wounds are healed.

God is a God of love, grace, and mercy. These attributes of His character are available to us because He is the omniscient One. He knows it all. First John 3:19–20 says, "This is how we know that we belong to the truth and how we set our hearts at rest in his presence: If our hearts condemn us, we know that God is greater than our hearts, and he knows everything."

Recognizing, biblically speaking, that a Christian may have a demon, and having considered the signs of how a believer could become demonized, let us turn our attention next to an examination of deliverance as part of a discipleship process that includes sanctification. I believe deliverance belongs to the church as part of the process of sanctification. Deliverance is not necessarily a one-time event, particularly if you remove the word *possession* and go back to the Greek meaning of *demonized* with its diversity of meaning.

Chapter 7

DELIVERANCE AS PART OF THE PROCESS OF SANCTIFICATION

———— ❦ ————

D R. VINSON SYNAN[1] IS DEAN OF THE SCHOOL of Divinity at Regent University in Virginia Beach, Virginia, and a historian of Pentecostalism. He belongs to the Pentecostal Holiness denomination. Pentecostal Holiness is sometimes called "three-stage" Pentecostalism, a differentiation from "two-stage" Pentecostalism. All the early Pentecostals except those with the Assemblies of God were three-stage Pentecostals. They believed in three stages of transformation: you were born again, justified, and then had a sanctification experience in which you gained power over sins that were besetting you. In the second stage you received the power not to transgress, or "sin," as part of this sanctification experience. Some would even use the word *perfected* to describe this; but as John Wesley put it, we are "perfected in love," not perfect.[2]

The Arminian definition of sin is that it is the purposeful, willful violation of the law of God,[3] which is also known as *high-handed sin*.[4] Their doctrine says that after you have a sanctification experience you can live your life free of high-handed sin, purposefully transgressing the law—premeditated transgression. The Reformed followers believed that sin was also error and ignorance, and falling short of the glory of God as revealed in Jesus. That is a much deeper understanding of sin, which deals with more than transgression.

Dr. Synan told me that, as a leading historian on Pentecostal Holiness, he has read many testimonies of people who he believes experienced deliverance in the process of sanctification. The Assemblies of God believe we are justified and that sanctification is not an event but a process that continues throughout the Christian life. The two stages are salvation and baptism in the Holy Spirit with sanctification not being an event but a process. Pentecostal Holiness people had these deliverance experiences even before being baptized in the Spirit. From his research of firsthand testimonies, Dr. Synan believes what was happening with some of these people was that they were being delivered. They were experiencing deliverance in the stage they called sanctification.

Now having said this, I believe the ministry of deliverance goes hand in hand with the church's teaching on sanctification. In my opinion, which comes from my own experience, deliverance is part of the process of sanctification. Confronting error with truth is an integral part of the process of inner healing that takes place through deliverance in the midst of sanctification.

Often the root cause of our problems is a lie that we believe, given to us by a demonic reality. When we believe a lie, it has power. Some deliverance happens through truth encounters and some through power encounters, because when God's truth is brought to bear on the lies of the enemy, the lies lose their power. And other times the problem isn't due to believing a lie; it comes from not knowing the truth that's necessary to walk in freedom.

Let's now turn our attention to an examination of the aspect of curses, inner vows, soul ties, and generational curses as they impact deliverance ministry.

Chapter 8

CURSES, INNER VOWS, SOUL TIES, AND GENERATIONAL CURSES

———————

I N BRAZIL MY FRIEND TOM HAUSER WAS TOUCHED one night by the power of the Holy Spirit. Authority over the demonic realm was given to him as we prayed over him. Hauser received a powerful fresh baptism of the Holy Spirit that resulted in a strong gift of discerning of spirits and authority for the ministry of deliverance. At the service that evening was a woman named June whose right leg was turned a full ninety degrees out toward the right. As Tom interviewed her, he found out that before June was born, her mother and father had a neighbor whose daughter's leg was also turned ninety degrees toward the right. June's father had mocked and derided the neighbor's child, causing the neighbor to speak a curse over June's mother when she was pregnant with June. When June was born, she had the same deformity.

The neighbor who spoke the curse was involved in Macumba witchcraft. I believe it was this curse that brought an evil spirit upon the mother and June, while she was unborn, causing the deformity of her leg. As Tom ministered deliverance, which was a process that took two nights, those of us on the team watched the foot and leg turn, 90 percent the first night and the remaining 10 percent the second night. All of the bones moved; everything shifted. As the demonic spirit was dealt with, the curse was broken and June was healed.

The ministry of deliverance often can involve the breaking of inner vows, curses, soul ties, and generational curses. The words we speak and the words spoken over us have more power than we realize.

CURSES

A curse is an evil appeal for harm to come to someone. Many of us are unaware that words of criticism or condemnation spoken to or about another can actually curse that person. When we speak against someone, we open a door for the demonic to exercise their legal right to attach to that person's life. Something said in anger or frustration can set in motion forces in the supernatural that have the potential to do great harm. Most people are unaware of this dynamic until they come under teaching that brings it to light. This is one category of curses.

The other major category is a purposeful curse spoken by someone who is operating in the occult with the intention of doing harm. Derek Prince has written an excellent book on the subject, titled *Blessing or Curse*, which I recommend reading. It gives a much more in-depth examination of the subject.[1]

In 1996 I was ministering in Argentina and had the privilege of working with Pastor Victor Lorenzo. He related the story of ministering deliverance to a woman who had made a blood covenant to destroy the church. Victor's father was preaching when this woman began to manifest violently, flying up into the air, breaking chairs, and causing a commotion. Victor's father had never encountered anything like this before and was taken aback by the manifestations.

It took the ministry team several days of working with this woman before they were able to uncover the root cause of her demonization. She confessed that she had made seven blood pacts, the first of which was when she was two years old. The seventh blood covenant she had made was to destroy the church.

Victor explained that there are different kinds of blood pacts. Some are made with the person's own blood, some with the blood of sacrificed animals, and some with the blood of sacrificed humans, particularly babies. This woman had made blood pacts with animal blood.

She was infested with six different demons. One appeared to be the leader and called itself Prince. As the ministry team worked with her, the demons would talk in all sorts of different voices and languages, sometimes in German, sometimes Hebrew, and sometimes English. This woman knew none of the languages. One particular demon would call out, "Joulen, Joulen, Joulen," as if it was trying to establish communication with another demon. After inquiring around, the ministry team found out there was an association of witches south of Buenos Aires that called themselves Joulens. They surmised that this particular demon might have been calling out to the ruling spirit over the entire area.

This woman renounced all the blood covenants. After she was delivered, the church ministered inner healing to her for several months to help her reintegrate into a healed lifestyle.

SEVEN SIGNS OF A CURSE

In the ministry of deliverance you will encounter both unintentional and intentional curses. The impact of them can range from moderate to severe. Many people do not know how to recognize that they have been cursed or how to fend off these fiery darts of the enemy. Derek Prince lists seven indications of a curse:

1. Mental and/or emotional breakdown

2. Repeated or chronic sickness (especially if hereditary)

3. Barrenness, a tendency to miscarry, or related female problems

4. Breakdown of marriage and family alienation

5. Continuing financial insufficiency

6. Being accident prone

7. A history of suicides and unnatural and untimely deaths[2]

Derek remarked, "When I compared my list with that of Moses, in Deuteronomy 28, I was impressed by the close correspondence between them."[3]

When you find yourself ministering to someone who is being delivered from a curse, I recommend using this faith response written by Derek:

> Lord, I desire to be set free from any curses over my life. I will do whatever it takes to be delivered from them and walk in the freedom You purchased for me.[4]

INNER VOWS

Inner vows are ones we make against ourselves. Most are not made with the intention of doing harm to ourselves. An inner vow can be the result of a hurt. In order to protect ourselves, we resolve never to let that same thing happen by making a vow that actually harms us instead of protecting us. One of the most common examples that all of us have probably seen at one time or another is the person who gets hurt in a relationship and vows never to get close to anyone again. They can end up bitter and lonely, living out the words they spoke. Or there is the person who does poorly at something and vows never to try again—becoming a failure.

These types of inner vows can lead to a life of desolation, but there are other types that can do far more damage, such as a person vowing that they want to die as a result of pain in their life.

When we lead someone through the process of renouncing previous or current involvement in any occult or cultic practices, they are breaking inner vows and pacts with the devil. For those involved in the occult, this renunciation is a prerequisite to the declaration that Jesus is Lord of all. We will examine occult practices in a little more depth in another chapter.

If you encounter a situation in which someone needs to renounce occult involvement, I recommend using this prayer:

> *In the name of Jesus I renounce any involvement in* [name the occult or cultic practice].
> *I renounce* [list all practices you participated in]. *I ask God to forgive me for worshipping other gods. I declare that Jesus is the way, the truth, and the life; no one comes to the Father but through Him. Jesus is Lord of all. I will worship God and Him alone.*

SOUL TIES

Soul ties are another form of bondage to the devil. Soul ties come about when we bond our flesh to the flesh of another in ungodly sexual relationships. Since restoration of the soul is the intention of the Lord, there must be a way to bring restoration to the soul that has been fragmented in unholy soulish relationships. Based on the intention of God for soul restoration and the dilemma of soul fragmentation by unholy sexual unions, we can deduce that God grants permission and authority to call our souls into holy alignment. With this assumption, we can confidently ask God to restore our souls into wholeness, restoring what was lost or given away that rightfully belongs to us, and sending away what is not ours to keep.

Here is the prayer my ministry teams use for the breaking of soul ties:

> *In the authority of Jesus I plead the blood of Jesus to stand between me and* [name the person] *and separate the "one flesh" union. I send back to him/her everything that I have taken from him/her when I became "one flesh" with him/her. I call back to me everything that I gave in this "one flesh" union. I declare the blood of Jesus to be a wall of separation between us. Thank You, Jesus, for restoring my soul.*

GENERATIONAL CURSES

Generational curses can descend on us through no fault of our own and wreak havoc until they are broken. A family member somewhere on the family tree who was involved in the occult, a curse spoken over a family, or sinful activity by someone on the family tree are all ways that generational curses can take root in our lives. These curses are open doors for the demonic. This is the prayer we use to break generational curses:

In the name of Jesus I declare the blood of Jesus to stand between me and the [name] generation as a wall of separation. I cancel every assignment of darkness and remove every right of the demonic to afflict me because of the sin of that generation. I call to me my righteous inheritance and the blessings of that generation.

Sometimes a curse begins in a family line as a cause-and-effect situation that sets up a predisposition to act and react in a certain way not in line with the will of God. This wrong reaction gets passed down from generation to generation and becomes like a curse that must be renounced and broken for the person to be set free. I believe all things demonic were dealt with on the Cross, including generational curses, but we must appropriate the benefits of the finished work of Christ for ourselves in order to receive their benefit.

BONDAGE AND THE POWER OF SUGGESTION

When we believe something, we empower it. We see this most often in cultures that practice voodoo. A shaman or witch doctor will speak something over a person, and because that person believes it, what was spoken will come about, even though there is no natural explanation for it. Although in such a case the supernatural power of evil can be at work, it sometimes is simply the power of suggestion at work—setting itself up to such a degree in a person that it causes their body to respond negatively.

This power of suggestion happens in our own culture as well. We have all heard of the placebo effect—when someone is given what they believe is medicine, when in fact it is nothing more than a sugar pill, and they experience a positive reaction. The opposite of the placebo effect is called the nocebo effect. If a person believes something negative, their belief can actually cause them harm. Perfectly healthy people can inadvertently be given a wrong diagnosis by their doctor and actually begin to suffer that wrong diagnosis. I recall reading of an instance where one person actually died when given a diagnosis of terminal cancer when they were in fact perfectly healthy.

We need to understand that it is our birthright to be free from the bondage of the curse of words.[5] God's blessings are more than sufficient to overcome any words spoken, to break any pact or vow taken, and to break any unholy soul tie entered into and cut off any generational sin passed down. We have been redeemed from every evil thing by the shed blood of Jesus on the cross. His sacrificial death gives us the means and the right to live free from the enemy's grip.

Let us now turn our attention to an examination of Satan and his demons.

Chapter 9

SATAN AND DEMONS

—— ❦ ——

To more fully understand our authority in the ministry of deliverance, it is important that we understand our adversary so we may appropriate the strategies of God in the midst of battle.

Satan and his minions are real, malevolent beings. God reveals Satan's identity to us clearly in the Scriptures. In the Old Testament God gives the prophet Isaiah a vision of Satan and a revelation of his nature.[1] In the New Testament Jesus confirms Isaiah's vision in the Gospel of Luke.[2] And then God again reveals and confirms Satan's identity to the apostle John in the Book of Revelation.[3] Both Jesus in Luke and John in Revelation make reference to the demons who were cast out of heaven with the devil.

What the Bible Tells Us

In Luke Jesus reminds the apostles that their authority to subdue evil spirits comes from Him. Then He goes on to tell them that the work of the kingdom, while important, does not overshadow their salvation. They are to rejoice that their names are written in heaven! We are nothing outside of our citizenship in heaven. It is from this position, seated with Jesus in heavenly places,[4] that all ministry flows. When we minister deliverance lovingly, with the heart of Christ, the "in-breaking" of His kingdom comes on earth.

In Revelation we are given a powerful picture of how Satan and his fallen angels were once cast out of heaven and will again, at the end of the age, be cast out once and for all. "The great dragon was hurled down—that ancient serpent called the devil, or Satan, who leads the whole world astray. He was hurled to the earth, and his angels with him" (Rev. 12:9; see also Rev. 20:10). Satan's intense hostility toward the people of God is clear, but so is God's authority and victory over the accuser.

The historic view of the church regarding demons is that they are fallen angels. They are identified as such in Revelation 12:4, 9. Verse four says that a third of the angels in heaven were flung to the earth. Because we know there are a large number of angels in heaven—"numbering thousands upon thousands, and ten thousand times ten thousand"[5]—we can deduct that one-third would mean there are a great many fallen angels at Satan's beck and call. The flip side of this picture is that there are a great many more angels in heaven who are available to assist us. The enemy is out-numbered two to one and underpowered, and we need to understand this. This is part of our identity in Christ, who is our hope of glory![6] Our understanding of this identity is essential in equipping us for ministry.

HIERARCHY AND ORGANIZATION

In the Book of Daniel we find reference both to God's angels, who assist us in battling Satan, and to a hier-archy in the demonic realm. In chapter 10 Daniel records his vision of "a man" sent from heaven in response to Daniel's prayers. In the midst of the vision the man spoke to Daniel about the prayers and petitions he had made on behalf of the Jews who were struggling to rebuild the temple. He explained why he had been delayed in answering Daniel's prayers: "But the prince of the Persian kingdom resisted me twenty-one days. Then Michael, one of the chief princes, came to help me, because I was detained there with the king of Persia" (Dan. 10:13). Biblical scholars believe the prince of Persia was a demon who was exercising his influence over the Persian kingdom. It took twenty-one days to overcome him, which indicates this was no ordinary demon, but one with great power. Clearly there is a hierarchy in the realm of Satan.

There are several passages in which the apostle Paul lists what appears to be a hierarchy within the realm of dark, evil beings. Demons appear to be the lowest among the ranks. In Colossians 1:16 Paul lists the governmental order of heavenly beings from which the evil beings fell with Satan: "For in him [Jesus] all things were created: things in heaven and on earth, visible and invisible, whether thrones or powers or rulers or authorities; all things were created by him and for him." Then in Colossians 2:15 Paul refers to their defeat by Christ on the cross: "And having disarmed the powers and authorities, he made a public spectacle of them, triumphing over them by the cross."

In Ephesians Paul further describes the divisions and qualifies these evil beings: "For our struggle is not against flesh and blood, but against the rulers, against the authorities, against the powers of this dark world and against the spiritual forces of evil in the heavenly realms" (Eph. 6:12). God did not establish these thrones, powers, rulers, and authorities of evil, because God is not the author of evil.

Often in deliverance ministry we will encounter multiple demons at work in a person's life, rather than a single demon. This indicates that demons are organized. We have found that when there is a group, there is typically a leader, which means they work under authority.

This also indicates hierarchy. These disembodied, living spirits speak, sometimes shouting or growling at us. They also screech, wail, and express fear ("Don't hurt me!") when confronted with the presence of Jesus in us. They do all of this to humiliate and to intimidate.

One of our goals in deliverance ministry is to rob the demonic of every opportunity to humiliate. If they begin to speak, we command them to be silent. If they start causing bizarre physical manifestations in the person, we command them to stop immediately in the name of Jesus. If they persist, we are more persistent. We never want to allow the demonic to be in control during deliverance. In the hierarchy of the ministry of deliverance Jesus is always the supreme authority. He is the matchless King who rules and reigns over all.

FORMS

The demonic can take many different forms. I was ministering with a team once, praying for a woman who was in pain from an afflicting spirit. As we commanded the spirit to leave her in the name of Jesus, we saw with our physical eyes (not our spiritual eyes) a green blob about the size of a small loaf of bread come out of her arm, move down her body and onto the floor, and then move across the floor and out of the building. On another occasion I saw a woman slither like a snake across the floor, contorting her body in ways that are impossible in the natural. Often people begin to hiss or spit as demons manifest.

SIN: AN OPEN DOOR

Our adversary the devil wants to destroy us, to cause us to self-destruct. He and his demons look for a legal "right" to attach to us, and when we sin we grant them this opportunity. Sin is the inroad for the demonic. Unresolved sin leads to enslavement to the devil. A point of enslavement is what we call a stronghold. If we give ground to the kingdom of darkness through sin, even though we have given our lives to Jesus, the demonic will think they have a legal right to attach to us through the sin. These attachments can come by our own choice, or by neglect or deception. The Bible clearly warns us not to give the devil a foothold.[7]

My friend Argentinian Pastor Victor Lorenzo told me the story of how he unwittingly gave a foothold to the devil and the impact it had on his family and his ministry. When his son Gonzalo was a year old, he began to experience what we often call "night terrors." Gonzalo would wake up in the middle of the night, around midnight, shouting and screaming, and nothing could calm him. This would go on until about 4:00 a.m. Victor and his wife began to fast and pray, but the night terrors continued. Then they got their church to fast and pray, but to no avail.

Finally Victor went before the Lord and asked God to speak to him. To his surprise God told Victor that he was guilty of resisting His call on his life. At the time, Victor was wrestling with what he was supposed to do with his life. His resistance had given space to the enemy.

Repentant, Victor asked the Lord to reveal the source of his son's night terrors. The next night, when the terrors began, Victor went into his son's room and as he did he felt a deep darkness. Fear came over him so strongly that it took his breath away. As he looked toward his son's crib, he saw a demon standing by the crib; it had the spirit of death on it. It was reaching for his son. His son was standing up in his crib pointing at the demon and screaming.

As Victor began to rebuke the demon in the name of Jesus, something like a bolt of lightning crashed through the room. He felt himself flying through the air, and when he regained his senses he was lying facedown on the floor and couldn't get up. An amazing presence came over the room. After what seemed like an hour, Victor was able to get up.

He went to his son's crib and found the child sleeping peacefully. Standing next to the crib was a large angel. The angel spoke to Victor and said, "I will be here to protect your children and your family." As a young child Gonzalo would tell his father how he would talk and pray with the angel, and how they would sometimes take the stairs up and back to heaven.

CONQUERED ON THE CROSS

While the demonic may view themselves as legal, we must view them as illegal squatters who have no right in the life of a believer. They are to be evicted through the finished work of the Cross. The devil does not play fair. He is a cheat, a liar, a thief, and a murderer, and if he thinks he has a right, he will claim it. He is a legalist looking for a loophole, and he will seize what he can.

We must reinforce what Jesus bought and paid for on the cross. The shed blood of the Cross destroyed the works of the devil and removed the curse of the law. Demons are trespassers. We are to serve them an eviction notice and remove them immediately from the premises. This is within our jurisdiction as believers. Both Satan and his demons are limited, but God has no limits. God is omnipresent, omniscient, and omnipotent. Satan is not.

In the Olivet Discourse of Matthew 24 and 25 Jesus teaches that at the end of the age He will come again in glory to gather all nations to Him. He will put those on His right who are to take their inheritance—"the kingdom prepared for you since the creation of the world"[8]—and those on His left who will be consigned to the fire—"Depart from me, you who are cursed, into the eternal fire prepared for the devil and his angels."[9] God gives this same revelation to the apostle John in great detail in Revelation 20:7–15, describing Satan's demise in verse 10: "And the devil, who deceived them, was thrown into the lake of burning sulfur, where the beast and the false prophet had been thrown. They will be tormented day and night for ever and ever."

God's power has no limits. Satan's power is limited. God's reign will never end, but Satan's will. His ultimate doom is clearly in the hands of God.

Chapter 10

THE OCCULT AND DEMONIZATION

THE OCCULT IN ALL ITS VARIOUS FORMS IS something we have to deal with frequently in deliverance ministry. The word *occult* in Greek means "to conceal from, to keep secret."[1] It is associated with the practice of magic, alchemy, astrology, divination, and necromancy, to name a few.

The Hebrew transliteration of the word *occult* comes from eight original Hebrew words, all of which pertain to the occult. They have to do with making contact with spirits that are not of God, making contact with the dead (necromancy), foretelling the future by casting lots, predicting the future from signs interpreted from nature, enchanting (as snake charmers do), casting spells by tying "magic" knots, evil sorcery, and speaking spells and curses over people.

The Bible has quite a lot to say about occult practices, both in the Old Testament and the New Testament.[2]

In Deuteronomy God warns the Israelites about occult practices:

> When you enter into the land which the LORD your God gives you, you must not learn to practice the abominations of those nations. There must not be found among you anyone who makes his son or his daughter pass through the fire, or who uses divination, or uses witchcraft, or an interpreter of omens, or a sorcerer, or one who casts spells, or a spiritualist, or an occultist, or a necromancer. For all that do these things are an abomination to the LORD.
>
> —DEUTERONOMY 18:9–12, MEV

Some historians surmise that "passing through the fire" was most likely an ancient coming-of-age ritual that involved a child running between two fires,[3] while other historians feel there is evidence that some practiced child sacrifice to the idol Molech and referred to it as "passing through the fire."[4]

In Acts 19:11–20 we find the story of a revival that broke out in Ephesus after a demonstration of God's power to heal. Paul was in the region with his disciples when "God did extraordinary miracles...so that even handkerchiefs and aprons that had touched him [Paul] were taken to the sick, and their illnesses were cured and the evil spirits left them" (Acts 19:11–12). There were some Jews in the area, the sons of Sceva, a Jewish chief priest who tried to drive out evil spirits by invoking the name of Jesus over the demon possessed (Acts 19:13–14). But the evil spirits, recognizing that these men were not followers of Jesus, overpowered them, beat them, and ran them off, naked and bleeding (Acts 19:15–16).

When word of this spread in Ephesus, "They were all seized with fear, and the name of the Lord Jesus was held in high honor. Many of those who believed now came and openly confessed what they had done. A number who had practiced sorcery brought their scrolls together and burned them publicly" (Acts 19:17–19). The Scripture goes on to say that the price of these scrolls equaled fifty thousand drachmas. (One drachma was equal to a day's wage.) It is likely that this high price was not due to the value of the scrolls but to their supposed occult power.[5]

In 1 Timothy Paul addresses the issues of demonic influence with his spiritual son Timothy: "Now the Spirit expressly says that in latter times some will depart from the faith, giving heed to deceiving spirits and doctrines of demons" (1 Tim. 4:1–2, NKJV). We are seeing this throughout the world today.

Again in Ephesians Paul counsels the church on how they are to stand against the devil: "Put on the full armor of God, so that you can take your stand against the devil's schemes. For our struggle is not against flesh and blood, but against the rulers, against the authorities, against the powers of this dark world and against the spiritual forces of evil in the heavenly realms" (Eph. 6:11–12).

FORMS OF THE OCCULT TODAY

Occult practices have made significant inroads into the fabric of life in the West, and many Christians are unaware this is happening. Whenever someone either knowingly or unknowingly participates in occult-based practices, they have opened a door, giving the demonic legal entry. I want to briefly examine some of the forms that the occult takes today in the twenty-first century.

Medicine. The most striking inroads into Western culture by the occult have been made in the field of medicine. Aberrant forms of healing with occult roots, often labeled as "alternative medicine," have gained a significant foothold in the practice of allopathic medicine beginning in the twentieth century. This has allowed the field of medicine in particular to become an open door for the devil to come into Western society, with the nursing profession, specifically, used as the road in.

"Conservative estimates are that close to 100,000 nurses have been trained to perform the technique called Therapeutic Touch,"[6] which has found its way into the health care curriculum of over eighty universities and colleges.[7] Research into Therapeutic Touch is funded by US government entities such as the National Institutes of Health and the US Department of Health and Human Services.[8] We are not talking about a few scattered practitioners with little credibility, but a well-organized effort to integrate the practice of medicine in the West.

Energy healing. Both Therapeutic Touch and Reiki have roots in Hinduism and Buddhism. Reiki therapy draws little support from the findings of natural science, and has no basis of support in Christian belief.[9] Rooted in Tibetan Buddhism, Reiki practitioners claim to channel universal-life energy into the body. With a mind of its own, this energy "knows" where to go to target places in the body in need of healing. Therapeutic Touch is rooted in spiritualism, the occult worldview, and especially Theosophy, a nineteenth century anti-Christian religious philosophy developed in New York by Madame Helene Blavatsky. Therapeutic Touch claims the ability to detect and manipulate a person's energy fields, thereby promoting self-healing. My book *Healing Energy: Whose Is It?*[10] provides in-depth information about New Age energy-healing modalities and their energy sources.

The word *reiki* can be loosely translated in Japanese to mean "god's life-force energy." It is important to remember that neither Buddhism nor Hinduism believes in the God of Christianity. Buddhism is non-theistic, meaning that it does not believe in any kind of god but instead teaches followers to seek truth through enlightenment and union with nature. Some of these occult healing practices are often thinly disguised as Christian healing and are duping unwitting believers and nonbelievers alike. You may encounter this deception when ministering deliverance.

New Age. The Catholic Church offers a well-researched overview of the "complex phenomenon of 'New Age'...which is influencing many aspects of contemporary culture" in a study by the Pontifical Council for Culture & Pontifical Council for Interreligious Dialogue titled *Jesus Christ, The Bearer of the Water of Life, A Christian reflection on the "New Age."*[11] It states, in part: "Inasmuch as health includes a prolongation of life, New Age offers an Eastern formula in Western terms"[12]—giving us practices such as acupuncture, biofeedback, reflexology, meditation, and reincarnation therapies to name a few, all of which promote the concept that our source of healing is not God but inner energy or cosmic energy.

Hungry for answers in an increasingly complex and challenging world, people eagerly reach out for these alternative practices and in the process they can receive more than they bargained for. When pantheistic energy from New Age practices is channeled into a person's body it brings along with it spirits of the occult.

Allopathic medicine. Modern allopathic medicine has failed to address the whole person, body, soul, and spirit, focusing instead only on the physical. This failure has left many who are in need of healing hungry for more. When we add together the failure of modern medicine to adequately address the whole person and the failure of the church to fully embrace the ministry of healing, including deliverance, we are left with a void that has been filled by New Age therapies.

I know a woman whose sister became demonized in one brief encounter with Reiki. An elementary school teacher, her sister happened to mention to the mother of one of her students that she was struggling with migraine headaches. The mother offered to "lay hands" on her using Reiki to help her with the migraines. Having no idea what Reiki was, she felt a bit uncomfortable with the suggestion but did not say no as hands were laid on her.

Soon afterward her migraines intensified, and she became quite ill. During prayer from a Christian friend she began to manifest somewhat violently. Her eyes rolled around in her head, she started jabbering in what sounded like an Asian language, and she began slapping the woman who was praying for her. Realizing that she was dealing with the demonic, her friend began to minister deliverance. When it was all over this young woman was delivered from several demons; they all identified themselves as Reiki demons.

Ouija, tarot, and video games. Even seemingly innocuous behavior such as using a Ouija board or tarot cards, or going to a fortune-teller "just for fun" can unwittingly open up a person to demonic power structures. Some of today's video games can become pathways to the occult. Be very mindful of what your children are doing. Most children have undeveloped spiritual discernment muscles with which to defend themselves. It is up to us to teach them the difference between good and evil. Satan does not play fair. He goes after children and will inflict as much damage as possible whenever he is given the opportunity. When we enter Satan's territory, willingly or unwittingly, we *will* get slimed.

Satanism. Those people who willingly participate in occult practices such as Satanism open themselves up to becoming highly demonized. They have taken blood oaths and made vows to Satan that are very challenging to break. The devil will do everything he can to keep them from slipping from his grasp, even going as far as killing them before they can be delivered.

The devil is the master of deception and will masquerade as goodness and light whenever possible. Holding fast to the Word of God will allow His spiritual light to reign in our hearts and minds and give us the discernment we need to unmask the devil's schemes. The Bible tells us that Satan will come as an angel of light.[13] He knows that the people of God are drawn to God's light, so he capitalizes on this to draw us into his darkness.

Satanic ritual abuse is the direct result of involvement in occult activities by adults who force their children to participate. Children seem to be among those most often abused. Many times, but not always, satanic ritual abuse experiences over a period of time will result in multiple personalities in the person who experienced them. This now is more often called Dissociative Identity Disorder and is a very serious matter. Counseling and prayers for a person so afflicted should only be done by those who have extensive professional training and experience. This can take hours, weeks, months, and in extreme cases sometimes years. Many times the person affected will not know they have multiple personalities until they go to a counselor.

For more information on this subject, including an extensive list of resources, I recommend Dr. Arlin Epperson's deliverance manual, *Healing of the Spirit: A Practical Manual for Deliverance and Inner Healing*, which can be found on his website www.healingofthespirit.org.

Freemasonry and secret societies. Secret occult societies such as Freemasonry, which masquerades as a good and worthy fraternal public service–oriented organization, have been a part of America since its inception. Because of the complex nature of Freemasonry we will examine it in detail in the next chapter.

Complementary health practices. I have ministered in Brazil for many years and have heard statistics that state approximately 80 percent of Brazilians have been to spiritist healers. I see the culture of the United States and Europe moving in that same direction with the advent of occult-based healing modalities in the practice of medicine. Let me say that not all complementary health practices are occultic. Many, although they are not based on Christian beliefs, fall into a neutral category. There are oils, vitamins, and natural nutritional supplements that are now used to complement our modern medical practices, and there is no reason I know of to consider them as potentially spiritually harmful.

Chiropractic medicine is a complementary health practice that requires discernment. It emerged in the late 1800s as an amalgamation of spiritualism, naturalism, magnetism, and vitalism, all of which believe in and rely on decidedly occultist premises. Today many chiropractors reject the original basis of chiropractic medicine in favor of a scientific viewpoint. This scientific viewpoint is based on research that has proved there are electrical impulses originating in the brain that travel through the spine. When these impulses are impeded by impingement of the nerves in the spinal cord, a person can experience health issues. Manual adjustment of the spine can alleviate impingement and bring relief.

Some chiropractors, even though they base their practice on scientific principles, also incorporate complementary therapies such as Reiki into their practice. Many of them are unaware of the dangers. In the process of deliverance ministry we may encounter those who have been demonized in this way, which is why it is important to give time and attention to the interview portion of the deliverance process to uncover what might otherwise remain hidden. Like chiropractic, acupuncture and acupressure may or may not be harmful, depending on the practitioner.

We in the West must be careful not to label everything Eastern as bad or harmful. While Eastern religions and certain Eastern medical practices have no room for the God of Christianity, we have to understand that Western allopathic medicine also has no room for God. What is spiritually harmful is what involves an anti-Christian worldview.

Chapter 11

FREEMASONRY

I N THE COURSE OF MINISTERING HEALING AND deliverance you will encounter those who are or have been involved in Freemasonry, or have Masonic influence in their ancestry.

In his book *Breaking Free* Tom Hauser says this about Freemasonry: "The original concept of the Scottish Rite Freemasonry was to develop a universal religion that people of any faith could accept and worship in...The Freemasonry 'god' is a combination of Jehovah, Baal, and Osiris, though this is not disclosed to members until they are somewhat advanced in the society."[1] Baal, according to occult literature, is one of the seven princes of hell, and Osiris was considered to be the ruler of the dead by ancient Egyptians. In addition to Freemasonry many contemporary occult practices continue to worship Baal and Osiris.

Freemasonry is characterized by secret rituals during which members must take secret oaths and vows that cannot be broken except under penalty of death. Any organization that requires members to take secret oaths and vows, however good and godly these oaths and vows may seem on the surface, should be strenuously avoided. Unwitting involvement in these organizations can lead straight into the devil's playground. The families of Freemasons can be found to suffer from excessive physical and emotional illness.

Freemasonry by its very nature is secretive, but much well-documented information exists from former members and from scholarly research by Christians. We do know that it appeared in Europe in the seventeenth century, specifically in England and Scotland where it remains strong today. Current estimates put worldwide membership at a little over three million.

European settlers brought Freemasonry to America, where it gained a significant foothold among our Founding Fathers. Many of our presidents were Masons, including George Washington. The Washington Monument in Washington, DC, is a phallic Masonic symbol. Similar Masonic monuments can be found in most major cities in the United States. Our currency is also adorned with Masonic symbolism such as the pyramid with the "all-seeing eye of spiritual light." Freemasonry is rife with anti-Christian symbolism that has its roots in occult worship, much of it sexually deviant worship. For this reason it is best to have women minister to women and men minister to men when dealing with the Masonic.

Almost every town and city in America has a Masonic lodge with the Masonic symbol prominently on display. The compass and level with the capital G in the center we are told represents the ancient art of stone making when in fact it is occult symbolism. Newly initiated Masons are told that the G stands for the "Great Architect of the Universe" who is their god.[2] They are told that their assignment is to embark on a quest to discover the real name of God. As they progress up through the levels of Freemasonry, it is not until they attain level seven that the "real" name of god is revealed.

> This name, "JAHBULON," is triune in blasphemous mockery of the true triune God of the universe. "JAH" is the shortened form of the Hebrew name "YAHWEH" or "JEHOVAH," which Christians know to be one of the names of God. "BUL" is another rendering of "BAAL," the pagan god of the Bible. "ON" was the word used to call upon the Babylonian deity "OSIRIS." This name is so sacred among the Masons that no Royal Arch Mason can pronounce the name alone. It takes three Masons to pronounce this "sacred" name. This name [JAHBULON] is used in further rites

and vows made by Masons in their climb up the Masonic pyramid.[3]

Once a person is invited to join a Masonic lodge they begin a progression through various degrees. Each degree requires the taking of secret oaths along with bizarre initiation practices designed to strip the person of their God-given identity and replace it with Satan's identity. As they progress through the degrees, occult idolatry increases until Satan himself becomes part of the initiation process. Great deception and confusion mingled with fear prevent most people from breaking free of Freemasonry on their own.

Initiation practices take place in the dark and can include the "noose around the neck," which symbolizes a mock hanging in which the person surrenders their mind to Freemasonry, being stripped of clothing, and the signing of oaths with their own blood. Penalties for breaking the oaths or revealing their secrets include dismemberment and death.

It is sad to know that so many have engaged in this type of absurd occult behavior for centuries with disastrous consequences, but it illustrates the depths of depravity of the mind of Satan and the degree to which he can deceive and enslave intelligent individuals. Most enter into Freemasonry unaware of its true identity until it is too late.

Barbara Cassada has an excellent book titled *Unto Death*,[4] which presents an in-depth understanding of Freemasonry and its satanic agenda. Chapter 6 of her book includes prayers for renunciation for all of the various degrees of Freemasonry. There are many other excellent books available regarding Freemasonry, some of which are listed in the back of her book. You can also find excellent information and a list of reading material in the online manual of Dr. Arlin Epperson.[5]

In the course of ministering healing and deliverance in their local church, Barbara and her husband, Bill, encountered those who were struggling to come out of Freemasonry. Then when they became acquainted with Global Awakening and began to travel world-wide as part of my ministry teams, they again began to encounter many instances of Freemasonry as they ministered healing and deliverance. With no prior knowledge of the Masonic, they researched the issue and were startled by what they found.

> What we discovered was diabolical and frightening in the intensity of its deception. Many situations we prayed for could be directly traced to the vows (curses) that Masons pronounce over themselves in each degree of elevation within

this secret society. As a Freemasons traverses the ladder of degrees from the very first oath as an Entered Apprentice, he binds himself forever more tightly to the diabolical schemes of the enemy. The Satanic rites are performed under the guise of following God, but when the light of truth is shined upon them, the reality of doctrine becomes crystal clear. The Word promises us that Satan will come as "an angel of light." In doing good for the community, the Freemasons and all attendant secret organizations following in its path (Mormonism, Elks, Shriners, Foresters, Moose, etc.) weave a web of deception that succors the heart of man into a loving fellowship and needed camaraderie, then binds that heart to itself with fear for the consequences of betrayal.[6]

Through Barbara and the work of others it has come to light that people involved in Freemasonry will very often exhibit specific infirmities as will their family members. Primary on the list are cancers, particularly of the colon, prostate, brain, and breast; Parkinson's disease; heart problems; mental health issues; and premature death of children and relatives.

As we examine some of the rites and vows/oaths involved in Freemasonry, keep in mind that these vows and oaths are in reality curses that individuals speak over themselves that carry over into the lives of their succeeding generations until those vows and oaths are renounced and broken by the power and authority of the name of Jesus Christ.

The Bible is very clear in its teaching on oaths. In Matthew Jesus tell us:

> Again, you have heard that it was said to the people long ago, "Do not break your oath, but fulfill to the Lord the vows you have made." But I tell you, do not swear at all: either by heaven, for it is God's throne; or by the earth, for it is his footstool; or by Jerusalem, for it is the city of the Great King. And do not swear by your head, for you cannot make even one hair white or black. All you need to say is simply "Yes" or "No"; anything beyond this comes from the evil one.
>
> —MATTHEW 5:38–42

First-Degree initiates into Freemasonry begin by taking secret vows in the midst of pagan rituals that swear on the name of God. As they progress through each succeeding level, the oaths and rituals take on greater obscenity and violence. Proverbs 18:21 tells us that the tongue holds the power of life and death. The Book of Exodus clearly tells us not to invoke the names of other gods or to let them be heard on our lips.[7]

A First-Degree initiate, called an "Entered Apprentice," swears to keep his vows, and should he violate these oaths in any way, he agrees to have his throat cut from ear to ear and his tongue torn out by the roots and buried in the sand at low tide. Advancing to the Second Degree as a "Fellow Craft," he swears to have his left breast torn open and his heart ripped out and given to the wild beats of the field and birds of the air if he violates his oath. A "Master Mason" at the Third Degree swears that if he should violate his oath he will consent to have his body cut in half, his bowels ripped out and burned after which they will be scattered to the wind. Part of the third-degree initiation process involved having the initiate lie on the floor as if dead so that the Worshipful Master can raise the person up to "new birth" in the Masonic. There are several degrees beyond the third degree but this brief examination is enough to help you understand the nature of the oaths and their resultant curses.

Masons are not to violate their oaths nor betray a fellow Mason except in cases of murder or treason. Barbara Cassada points out that the "murder and treason" wording was added to the oath after the death of former Freemason William Morgan in 1826.[8] Morgan left the Masons, and when he published the secrets of his lodge, he was murdered. Cassada goes on to point out the horrific implications of this when we consider that many in leadership in law enforcement and our judicial system, and at high levels of our government, are Freemasons. "Should a judge sitting on the bench receive the Masonic sign from a defendant, he finds himself more bound to his brother in the lodge than to the law which he has sworn to uphold. The same is true for law enforcement officers, lawyers, solicitors, barristers, etc., regardless of nationality. Wherever Freemasonry exists, loyalty to a fellow mason takes precedent over right and wrong."[9]

Barbara Cassada's book details the testimony of a man who broke free of Freemasonry as a result of attending one of Global Awakening's healing conferences in 1989.[10] As I (Randy Clark) taught on Freemasonry and deliverance, this man began to feel sick to his stomach. Confused and curious, he bought a copy of Cassada's book and read it the next day. The more he read, the sicker he became as the Holy Spirit began to convict him of the truth of Freemasonry.

As he began to renounce the oaths he had taken and cry out to God for forgiveness, demons literally began to tear his insides out. He said it felt as if cats were clawing his stomach and intestines. Feeling the need to vomit and relieve himself, he ran to the restroom. Once there he began bleeding profusely into the toilet. He battled throughout the day and into the next day. With the compassionate help of his wife and his pastor, he was eventually delivered and set free as he walked through hours of renouncing his involvement in Freemasonry. "I realized that for all those years spent in opposition to God, He was there all the time watching out for me, loving me, and longing for a relationship with me. I know that God revealed His love to me that day—forgave me of my sin and *set me free!*"[11]

None of the degrees of Freemasonry contain any spiritual truth to make them worthy of all of the curses and secrecy they contain. Quite the contrary, the secrecy serves to confuse, deceive, and hide the truth from anyone attempting to examine Freemasonry. The principles of Freemasonry are composed of select portions of the Christian faith placed on a decidedly anti-Christian foundation.

Because of the secret nature of Freemasonry and other similar secret societies, the web of deception they create is often difficult to recognize. When you encounter others who are suffering the consequences of the curses of Freemasonry, either through the oaths they have taken or from ancestral involvement in Freemasonry, it is imperative that they be walked through renunciation in order to cancel Satan's authority in their lives. Helping people gain freedom from Masonic influence should not be difficult if they are willing to pray renunciation prayers out loud and with sincerity of heart.

I recommend the following prayers of renunciation.

PRAYERS FOR FREEDOM FROM FREEMASONRY[12]

Have the seeker read the following prayer aloud. While this prayer is lengthy, the extra time is of little consequence to the benefit of assuring that all open gates are closed.

> *Father God, Creator of heaven and earth, I come to You in the name of Jesus Christ, Your Son. I come as a sinner seeking forgiveness and cleansing from all sins committed against You and others made in Your image. I honor my earthly father and mother and all of my flesh and blood ancestors, and also those of the spirit by adoption and godparents, but I utterly turn away from and renounce all their sins.*
>
> *I forgive all my relatives and ancestors for passing on the effects of their sins to me and to my children. I confess and renounce all of my own sins in this area as well. I renounce and rebuke Satan and every spiritual power*

of his that affects me and all members of my family, in the worthy name of Jesus.

I renounce and forsake all involvement in Freemasonry or any other lodge or craft by my ancestors, my relatives, and by myself. I renounce witchcraft, the principal spirit behind Freemasonry, and I renounce Baphomet—the spirit of antichrist and the curse of the Luciferian doctrine. I renounce the idolatry, blasphemy, secrecy, and deception of Masonry at every level. I specifically renounce the insecurity, the love of position and power, the love of money, avarice and greed, and the pride that led my ancestors into Masonry. I renounce all the fears that held them in Masonry, especially the fear of death, the fear of men, and the fear of trusting, in the precious name of Jesus Christ.

I renounce every position held in the lodge by myself and any of my ancestors, including "Tyler," "Master," "Worshipful Master," or any other. I renounce the calling of any man "Master," for Jesus Christ is my only master and Lord, and He forbids anyone else being called by that title. I renounce the entrapping of others into Masonry and observing *the helplessness of others during the rituals. I renounce the effects of Masonry passed on to me through any female ancestor who felt distrusted and rejected by her husband as he entered and attended any lodge and refused to tell her of his secret activities. I pray for all these favors in the blessed name of Jesus Christ, my Savior.*

First Degree

I renounce the oaths taken and the curses involved in the First (or Entered Apprentice) Degree, especially their effects on the throat and tongue. I renounce the hoodwink (the blindfold) and its effects on the emotions and eyes, including all confusion, fear of the dark, fear of the light, and fear of sudden noises. I renounce the secret word "boaz," and all it means. I renounce the mixing and mingling of truth and error, and the blasphemy of this degree of Masonry. I renounce the noose around the neck, the fear of choking, and also every spirit causing asthma, hay fever, emphysema, or any other breathing difficulty. I renounce the compass point, sword, or spear held against the breast, the fear of death by stabbing pain, and the fear of heart attack instilled from this degree.

I now pray for healing of the throat, vocal cords, nasal passages, sinuses, bronchial tubes, etc., for healing of the speech area, and the release of the Word of God to me and through me and all members of my family, in the name of Jesus Christ.

Second Degree

I renounce the oaths taken and the curses involved in the Second (or Fellow Craft) Degree of Masonry, especially the curses on the heart and chest. I renounce the secret words "jachin" and "shibboleth" and all that these mean. I cut off the emotional hardness, apathy, indifference, unbelief, and deep anger felt and experienced by me and all members of my family. I pray for the healing of my chest, lungs, and heart areas, and also for the healing of my emotions, and I ask that I be made sensitive to the Holy Spirit of God, in the name of Jesus Christ.

Third Degree

I renounce the oaths taken and the curses involved in the Third (or Master Mason) Degree, especially the curses on the stomach and womb area. I renounce the secret words "maha bone," "machaben," "machbinna," and "tubal cain," and all that they mean. I renounce the spirit of death from the blows to the head enacted as ritual murder, the fear of death and false martyrdom, the fear of violent gang attack, assault or rape, and the helplessness of this degree. I renounce the falling into the coffin (or stretcher) involved in the ritual of murder. I renounce the false resurrection of this degree, because only Jesus Christ is the Resurrection and the Life! I also renounce the blasphemous kissing of the Bible on a witchcraft oath. I cut off all spirits of death, witchcraft, and deception, and in the name of Jesus Christ, I pray for the healing of [naming those that apply] my stomach, gall bladder, womb, liver, and any other organs of my body affected by masonry, and I ask for a release of compassion, understanding, and forgiveness for me and my family. I pray for all these favors in the blessed name of Jesus Christ.

Holy Royal Arch Degree

I renounce and forsake the oaths taken and the curses and iniquities involved in the Holy Royal Arch Degree of Masonry, especially the oath regarding the removal of the head from the body and the exposing of the brains to the hot sun. I renounce the Mark Lodge and the mark in the form of squares and angles that marks the person for life. I also reject the jewel, or talisman, which may have been made from this mark sign and worn at lodge meetings.

I renounce the false secret name of God, "Jahbulon," and declare total rejection of all worship of false pagan gods, namely Bul or Baal and On or Osiris. I also renounce the password, "ammiruhamah," and its occult meaning. I renounce the false communion or eucharist taken in this degree, and all the mockery, skepticism, and unbelief about the redemptive work of Jesus Christ on the cross at Calvary. I repent of and cut off all these curses and their effects upon me and my

*family, and I command healing of the brain
and the mind, in the name of Jesus Christ.*

Eighteenth Degree

*I renounce the oaths taken and the curses
involved in the Eighteenth Degree of Masonry,
the Most Wise Sovereign Knight of the Pelican
and the Eagle and Sovereign Prince Rose Croix
of Heredom. I renounce and reject the Pelican
witchcraft spirit, as well as the occult influence
of the Rosicrucians and the Kabbala in this
degree. I renounce the claim that the death
of Jesus Christ was a "dire calamity" and the
deliberate mockery and twisting of the Christian doctrine of the Atonement. I renounce the
blasphemy and rejection of the deity of Jesus
Christ and the secret words "igne natura ren-
ovaturintegra" and their meaning. I renounce
the mockery of the communion taken in this
degree, including a biscuit, salt, and white
wine, in the name of Jesus.*

Thirtieth Degree

*I renounce the oaths taken and the curses
involved in the Thirtieth Degree of Masonry,*

the grand Knight Kadosh and Knight of the
Black and White Eagle. I renounce the password, "stibiumalkabar," and all it means, in
the blessed name of Jesus.

Thirty-First Degree

I renounce the oaths taken and the curses
involved in the Thirty-First Degree of Masonry,
the Grand Inspector Inquisitor Commander. I
renounce all the gods and goddesses of Egypt,
which are honored in this degree, including
Anubis with the ram's head, Osiris the sun
god, Isis the sister and wife of Osiris, and
also the moon goddess. I renounce the Soul
of Cheres, the false symbol of immorality, the
Chamber of the Dead and the false teaching
of reincarnation, in the name of Jesus.

Thirty-Second Degree

I renounce the oaths taken and the curses
involved in the Thirty-Second Degree of
Masonry, the Sublime Prince of the Royal
Secret. I renounce masonry's false trinitarian
deity, AUM, and its parts: Brahma (the cre-
ator), Vishnu (the preserver), and Shiva (the

destroyer). I renounce the deity of Ahura-Mazda, the claimed spirit or source of all light, and the worship with fire (which is an abomination to God), and drinking from a human skull, as done in some societal rites, in the name of Jesus Christ.

York Rite

I renounce the oaths taken and the curses involved in the York Rite of freemasonry, including Mark Master, Past Master, Most Excellent Master, Royal Master, Select Master, Super Excellent Master, the Orders of the Red Cross, the Knights of Malta, and the Knights Templar degrees. I renounce the secret words of "joppa," "kebraioth," and "Maher-shalal-hashbaz." I renounce the vows taken on a human skull, the crossed swords, and the curse and death wish of Judas, of having the head cut off and placed on top of a church spire. I renounce the unholy communion and especially drinking from a human skull, as done in some societal rites, in the blessed name of Jesus Christ.

Shriners

I renounce the oaths taken and the curses and penalties involved in the Ancient Arabic Order of Nobles of the Mystic Shrine. I renounce the piercing of the eyeballs with a three-edged blade, the flaying of the feet, the madness, and the worship of the false god Allah, the god of our fathers. I renounce the hoodwink, the mock hanging, the mock beheading, the mock drinking of the blood of the victim, the mock dog urinating on the initiate, and the offering of urine as a commemoration, in the blessed name of Jesus Christ.

Thirty-Third Degree

I renounce the oaths taken and the curses involved in the Thirty-Third Degree of Masonry, the Grand Sovereign Inspector General. I renounce and forsake the declaration that Lucifer is God. I renounce the cable-tow around the neck. I renounce the death wish—that the wine drunk from a human skull should turn to poison—and the skeleton, whose cold arms are solicited if the oath of this degree is violated. I renounce the three infamous assassins of their Grand Master, law, property, and religion, and the greed and witchcraft involved in the attempt to manipulate and control the rest of mankind, in the blessed name of Jesus Christ.

All other degrees

I renounce all the other oaths taken, the rituals of every other degree, and the curses therein involved. I renounce all other lodges and secret societies, such as Prince Hall Freemasonry, Mormonism, the Order of Amaranth, Oddfellows, the Buffaloes, Druids, Foresters, Orange, Elks, Moose and Eagles Lodges, the Ku Klux Klan, the Grange, the Woodmen of the World, Rider of the Red Robe, the Knights of Pythias, the Mystic Order of the Veiled Prophets of the Enchanted Realm, the women's Orders of the Eastern Star and of the White Shrine of Jerusalem, the girls' Order of the Daughters of the Eastern Star, the International Orders of Job's Daughters and of Rainbow Girls, and the boys' Order of DeMolay, and their effects upon me and all members of my family, in the precious name of Jesus Christ.

I renounce the ancient pagan teaching and symbolism of the First Tracing Board, the Second Tracing Board, and the Third Tracing Board, as used in the rituals of the Blue Lodge. I renounce the pagan ritual of the "Point with a Circle" with all its bondages and phallus (penis) worship. I renounce the occult mysticism of the black and white mosaic checkered floor, with the tessellated (or adorned) pagan symbolism and bondages. I renounce and utterly forsake the Great Architect of the Universe, who is revealed in the higher degrees as Lucifer, and his false claim to be the universal fatherhood of God. I also renounce the false claim that Lucifer is the Morning Star and Shining One, and I declare that Jesus Christ alone is the Bright and Morning Star spoken of in Revelation 22:16.

I renounce the All-Seeing Third Eye of freemasonry or Horus in the forehead and its pagan and occult symbolism. I renounce all false communions, all mockery of the redemptive work of Jesus Christ on the cross at Calvary, all unbelief, confusion, and depression, and all worship of Lucifer as God. I renounce and forsake the lie of Freemasonry—that man

131

is not sinful, just imperfect, and so can redeem himself through good works. I rejoice that the Bible declares that I cannot do a single thing to earn my salvation, and that I can only be saved by grace through faith in Jesus Christ and what He accomplished on the Cross at Calvary.

I renounce all fear of insanity, and I renounce anguish, death wishes, suicide, and death, in the name of Jesus Christ. Death was conquered by Jesus Christ, and He alone holds the keys of death and health, and I rejoice that He holds my life in His hands even now. He came to give me life abundantly and eternally, and I believe in His promises.

I renounce all anger, hatred, murderous thoughts, revenge, retaliation, spiritual apathy, false religion, and unbelief, especially unbelief in the Holy Bible as God's Word, and all occasions of compromising God's Word. I renounce all spiritual searching into false religions and all my striving to please God, who already knows and loves me eternally. I rest in the knowledge that I have found my Lord and Savior, Jesus Christ, and that I am no more "lost" to Him—He has found me.

I will burn all objects in my possession that connect me with all lodges and occult organizations, including masonry and witchcraft, their regalia, aprons, books of rituals, rings, and other apparel and jewelry. I renounce the effects these (or other objects of masonry, such as the compass, the square, the noose, or the blindfold) have had upon me or any members of my family, in Jesus's blessed name.

Holy Spirit, I ask that You show me anything else I need to do or for which I need to pray, so that I and all members of my family may be totally free from the consequences of the sins of masonry, witchcraft, and paganism—and from any and all things unrighteous.

Now, Father God, I ask humbly for the blood of Jesus Christ Your Son to cleanse me from all these sins of which I have confessed and renounced, to cleanse my spirit, my soul, my mind, my emotions, and every part of my body that has been affected by these sins, in Jesus's holy name!

I renounce every evil spirit associated with masonry, witchcraft, and all other sins, and I command—in the name of Jesus Christ—for Satan and every evil spirit to be bound and to leave me now, touching or harming no one, and that they go to the place appointed by the Lord Jesus, never again to return to me or any member of my family. I call on the name of the Lord Jesus alone to be delivered of these spirits, in accordance with the many promises mentioned in the Bible. I ask to be delivered of every spirit of sickness, infirmity, curse, affliction, addiction, disease, or allergy associated with these sins of which I have confessed and renounced.

I surrender to God's Holy Spirit—and to no other spirit—all the places in my life where these sins have been. I ask You, Lord, to baptize me in Your Holy Spirit now, according to the promises of Your Word. I take to myself the whole armor of God in accordance with Ephesians chapter 6 and rejoice in its protection as Jesus surrounds me and fills me with the Holy Spirit.

I enthrone You, Lord Jesus, within my heart, for You are my Lord and my Savior, the source of eternal life. Thank You, Father God, for Your mercy, Your forgiveness, and Your life, in the name of Jesus Christ I pray. Amen.

Those who have actually been involved in the various degrees of Freemasonry are encouraged to symbolically do the following, as they read the prayer above.

- Symbolically remove the blindfold (hood-wink) and give it to the Lord for disposal.

- In the same way symbolically remove the veil of mourning.

- Symbolically cut and remove the noose from around the neck; gather it up with the cable-tow running down the body and give it all to the Lord for His disposal.

- Renounce the false Freemasonry marriage covenant, removing from the fourth finger of the right hand the ring of this false marriage covenant and giving it to the Lord to dispose of.

- Symbolically remove the chains and bondages of Freemasonry from your body.

- Symbolically remove all Freemasonry regalia and armor, especially the apron.

- Symbolically remove the ball and chain from the ankles.

- Repent of and seek forgiveness for having walked on unholy ground, including Freemasonry lodges and temples.

- Proclaim that Satan and his demons no longer have any legal right to mislead and manipulate you.

The following is a list of other secret societies under the Freemasonry umbrella that you may encounter in the course of ministering deliverance.

- Order of the Eastern Star
- Order of the White Shrine of Jerusalem
- Order of Amaranth
- Order of DeMolay
- Daughters of the Eastern Star
- Daughters of the Nile
- International Order of Job's Daughters
- International Order of Rainbow for Girls
- Shriners

Freedom in Christ through His finished work on the cross in the ministry of healing and deliverance is typically not straightforward. Dr. Epperson has this to say: "While many people seem to focus on one spiritual problem at a time, this usually is somewhat fruitless. A seeker, because of their own experiences as well as those that have been handed down from their ancestors (Exodus 20:5), will typically have a number of areas in their life that may have opened 'doors' for the influences of darkness to affect them. Most deliverance ministers will highly recommend a 'whole meal deal,' rather than a one-problem focus. Even if prayer removes the influence from the focused area, if the other areas are not dealt with as well, the problems in the focused area will return, through the areas which have not been dealt with."[13]

Chapter 12

MINISTERING DELIVERANCE

❈━━◆◆◆◆◆◆━━❈

MINISTERING DELIVERANCE IS NEVER THE same with any two people. You may proceed gently and quietly through one deliverance only to be faced with all sorts of bizarre manifestations in the next. When strong and unusual manifestations do occur, there are ways to deal with them to bring the situation under control, rather than leaving control in the hands of the demonic. When we minister from the heart of love as found in Jesus and the authority given to us by His finished work on the cross, deliverance ministry can be put into its proper perspective, which is to set the captives free.

Ministering healing and deliverance is not about adherence to a method. Methods provide information and guidelines, but it is the Holy Spirit who ultimately guides us when we minister. The method presented here provides an excellent foundational guideline for ministering deliverance, but it is only a guideline. Just as a surgeon may find himself in uncharted territory when he opens up a person on the operating table and encounters something he has never seen before, we may find ourselves in uncharted territory in the middle of deliverance. When this happens we must trust the Holy Spirit, because we know that it is God's desire for all to live in freedom.

To minister deliverance, we must be confident and clear in our identity and power as a child of the King and know how to walk in our authority in Jesus. What God calls us to, He will empower us to do. As Jesus taught His disciples to advance the kingdom of God, He modeled two things for them. He taught them how to declare and demonstrate the kingdom of God. The act of demonstrating the kingdom provided opportunity to declare the kingdom. Demonstration validated declaration.

Jesus's Authority Is Absolute

When we cast out demons we are demonstrating the kingdom of God.[1] We must learn to live convinced of the absolute victory of Jesus over the kingdom of darkness, convinced that Jesus has absolute authority in heaven and on earth.[2] We must understand that the devil has been stripped of all authority and dwell not on the devil but on the greatness of God: "And having disarmed the powers and authorities, he made a public spectacle of them, triumphing over them by the cross" (Col. 2:15). We must become secure in our authority in Jesus, understanding the principle of unification—that we are one with Jesus.[3] We died with Christ, were buried with Him, raised with Him, and are now seated with Him in heavenly places, and we have the right to walk out and exercise the authority given to us.[4] Here is the identity statement that I teach students who will be ministering deliverance:

- I am a child of the King. I am a coheir with Jesus.

- Everything Jesus bought and paid for is my inheritance.

- I am united with Jesus. I have been crucified with Christ.

- I died with Him. I was buried with Him.

- I was raised with Him.

- I am seated with Him in the heavenlies, far above all rule, all power, all authority, and above every name that is named, not only in this age, but also in the one to come.

- Therefore I carry the authority of Christ.

- I have authority over sickness, over sin, over the flesh, over demons, and over the world.

- I am the salt of the earth. I am the light of the world.

- I will displace the darkness. I have the full armor of God.

- I put on the breastplate of righteousness, the belt of truth, the helmet of salvation, the shoes of peace.

- I take up the shield of faith and the sword of the Spirit.

- For the weapons of my warfare are not fleshly.

- They are divinely powerful to tear down the strongholds of darkness.

- I can do all things through Christ, because greater is He who is in me than he who is in the world.[5]

Seeing a demon under every bush or behind every problem is not biblical, but neither is the denial of their existence or operation. Sadly many who could be helped, especially in Western societies, are denied assistance because of the lack of practical instruction or by theologies that deny their need. It is not unusual to read accounts of Western missionaries who quickly change their theology when confronted openly with demonic activity in the mission fields of Asia, Africa, and South America.

When revival hit Argentina in the mid-1990s, Pastor Pablo Bottari—an internationally recognized authority on the ministry of deliverance—was brought in, asked by theologians Pablo Deiros and Carlos Miranda to help. Both Dr. Deiros and Dr. Miranda were professors at the International Baptist Theological Seminary in Argentina at the time. Dr. Deiros was at one time a professor at Princeton Theological Seminary, and the first Hispanic to teach at that prestigious institution. During his tenure, a Toronto-like revival broke out. He resigned from Princeton to return home to his church.

The revival brought manifestations such as laughing and falling, shaking and being slain in the Spirit, along with demonic manifestations. Demonic manifestations are common during revival, and their prevalence in the Argentinian revival brought with it a great need to develop a model for ministering deliverance.

Bottari was a humble man with a unique anointing for ministering deliverance. He ministered with great compassion, exhibiting love, patience, and gentleness.

During crusades he could be found ministering late into the night so as not to overlook even one person oppressed by the devil. The ministry of deliverance as taught by Bottari was forged in the fires of experience, as he and his teams sought God's leading. They would be constantly on their faces before the Lord, praying to understand how He would have them go about the process of setting people free from the work of the enemy.

The authority of Bottari's teachings is based on his deep relationship with Jesus Christ and his practical application of Scripture under the guidance of the Holy Spirit. His humble, teachable spirit allows God to use him mightily. He describes it in his book *Free in Christ*:

> Each time I cried out to the Lord asking for wisdom, He always answered me. More than one million souls in bondage have received ministry in the deliverance tent, thirty thousand of whom I have personally dealt with, but my attitude has never changed. I have sought to humble myself before the Lord completely, to depend on the Holy Spirit absolutely and to believe in the authority He has given me as His own child.[6]

> This tent, which measured approximately 60 feet wide by 230 feet long, was filled every night with demonized people. Great patience was

143

needed to work in there. Loud screaming, tortured gestures and violent behavior were demonstrated by many.[7]

Local ministers labored for hours but were unable to set these dear ones free until Pablo Bottari took charge. Under his leadership people began to get delivered. Prayerfully seeking the strategies of God, with Jesus as their example, Bottari, Carlos Annacondia, and the other pastors were able over time to develop an effective model for deliverance based on Bottari's methods.

Bottari's ten-step model is quiet, pastoral, loving, and nonhumiliating. It is the basis for the model we use at all of our crusades and conferences, and on our international ministry trips—with great success.

As we examine this model in the next chapter, keep in mind that these guidelines provide information, but, like Bottari, your ability to minister deliverance also will develop over time from experience. We have found that the guidelines provided in this model can be used effectively whether you are ministering in a large setting such as a conference or crusade, in a small church setting, or one on one.

Chapter 13

GUIDELINES FOR MINISTERING DELIVERANCE

———◆———

PRAYING FOR DELIVERANCE IS SOMETHING THAT must be done with encouragement, acceptance, and love. To deliver someone, demons must be driven away and access doors closed to prevent the return of the evil spirits. Access doors can be opened by hurts, sins, and unforgiveness and will remain open if these feelings are not dealt with in a hopeful, loving way.

THE PERSON IS THE PRIORITY

When we minister deliverance, we are ministering to a person, not a demon. As you minister, counsel the person in order to bring forth the truth. Minister quietly, avoiding flamboyant demonstrations of warfare. Satan loves to make a scene and will try to humiliate and torment in the midst of deliverance. We want to rob him of every opportunity to do so. Bottari teaches: "Deliverance is not about shouting! It is focused on discovering what it is that is giving the enemy authority to remain in a person's life."[1]

Always give the individual priority. Recognize and be sensitive to the fact that the person you are praying for may have lost hope of being set free after having spent years in bondage. Remain faithful, steady, and comforting. Provide a loving, quiet environment for deliverance. Deliverance can be a long process. Do not try to rush through it.

TAKING AUTHORITY OVER MANIFESTATIONS

The next step in ministering deliverance involves recognition of manifesting spirits. If a spirit manifests, command it to be quiet and submit to you "in the name of Jesus." You take authority over a spirit when you order it to submit in Jesus's name. If the person you are praying for does not seem to understand the circumstances, reassure them that you are speaking to the spirit that is manifesting.

You must be persistent, as it can take time to command a spirit. It must submit eventually, so maintain faith. Dr. Epperson says that demons tend to know how much faith you have, just as dogs know if you have fear. Make sure not to stir the spirit by touching or speaking loudly to the person in bondage. Your goal is to quiet the spirit, not stir it up.

Make sure that you establish and maintain communication with the person to whom you are ministering. Remain calm and loving. Encourage the person. Ask them if they can hear you. If they cannot hear you or respond to you when asked to do things, another spirit may be present, and you must command authority over it in the name of Jesus.

The spirit may manifest by causing the person you are praying for to growl, whine, argue, threaten, or contort. Do not speak to the spirit unless it is to command it to submit in the name of Jesus. Ministry should be done in a quiet place where there is little distraction. Maintain authority and communicate clearly.

DETERMINING SINCERITY

When you have quieted any manifesting spirits and established communication with the person, it is time to ask them if they want to be free and to determine if they are sincere in their request to be set free. They must be sincere or the bondage can and will likely return. If you find that the person does not want deliverance and wants to continue with the lifestyle holding them in bondage, do not pray for deliverance. Provide love and encouragement and end the session until they truly wish to be set free.

ACCEPTING JESUS AS LORD AND SAVIOR

If the person is sincere and earnestly desires to be set free, then it is time to ask them if they have accepted Jesus as their Lord and Savior. This is important because if they are a believer, the Holy Spirit will help them stay free. If they are not a believer, bondage can and likely will return. If they are not a believer, offer to lead them to Christ. If you cannot, then bless them instead and encourage them to continue to consider accepting Jesus as Lord.

If the person you are praying for truly wants to be set free and is a believer who has accepted Jesus, then you are ready to proceed to the interview phase. In this phase you will attempt to explore what has led to the person's bondage by revealing open access doors through which the enemy has entered the person's life.

THE INTERVIEW PHASE

Begin the interview process with questions about relationships, specifically about the person's mother and father, and continue from there. Look for areas where forgiveness may be necessary, where repentance may help break bondage. Look for hurts, sins, feelings of rejection, or fear. Seek to learn more about what the person's parents were like. Ask questions such as, "How did they treat each other?"

Any hurts that are revealed will need to be acknowledged and forgiven. Consider whether a curse is involved if the person has persistent difficulty in an area of life. Also, remember that fear is an entry point for many different spirits and an underlying problem in many illnesses. Do not stir up demons. Keep them quiet.

Look for open doors stemming from areas such as sex, trauma, addiction, curses, emotions, illness, or the occult. Do not hurry this process; be patient, looking for demonic manifestations and the open doors they are coming through.

CLOSING THE DOORS

When you feel that the Holy Spirit has revealed everything, you are ready to begin closing the open doors. If possible during the interview process, have someone keep notes of all the doors that need to be closed. Remember, only one person should minister deliverance. All other team members should pray silently.

When you believe you have determined what the open access doors are, it is time to begin the process of closing those doors. Seek to close *all* doors, leaving nothing open for oppression.

The process of closing doors always begins with forgiveness.[2] Rather than asking the person whom they need to forgive, ask them what hurts they have. Start by having the person forgive all those who have hurt them. It is important to be specific. Because it can often be painful to relive past hurts, provide comfort, hope, protection, and love. When every hurt has been forgiven, ask the person you are praying for to open their mind to any other hurts the Holy Spirit may still want to show them.

After all hurts have been revealed and forgiven, have the person release to God each and every person who has hurt them. If the person you are praying for is unable to forgive, do not proceed with deliverance; forgiveness must be given in order to be received. Bondage can be broken only when forgiveness is given.

FORGIVENESS FOR SINS

If the person is able to forgive others, then they are ready to take the next step, which is to seek forgiveness for their own sins. Feelings such as anxiety, anger, resentment, or pride must be dealt with because they are open doors to oppression. If any of these feelings are present, ask the person to repent, giving these feelings to God. They will receive forgiveness through this process of confession and repentance.

RENOUNCING AND BREAKING YOKES

After you have progressed through the forgiveness phase, it is time to have the person renounce in the name of Jesus all sins or spirits involved. This is the time when they must renounce all sex partners outside of marriage; and any inner vows, pacts, or curses must be renounced and broken. Renunciation must be audible and spoken firmly; renunciation is not a prayer to God but a command spoken to an enemy.

Remain persistent and patient as you close all doors that could lead to future bondage. The person ministering deliverance should break the yoke of bondage and the power of any spirit. This closes the door. Declare, for example: "In the name of Jesus I break the power of the spirits(s) of [name the spirit(s)] over [name] so that when they are cast out, they will not come back."

CASTING OUT SPIRITS

You now are ready to cast out unclean spirits. Sometimes a person will indicate that the spirit is leaving by burping, yawning, jerking, or wincing. If the person you are praying for starts to manifest or is strained in some

151

way, all doors may not be closed. Ask the Holy Spirit for help. Check with the person and ask if any doors are still open. They may know. If doors are still open, stop and seek to close all doors before commencing to cast out unclean spirits.

INVITING THE HOLY SPIRIT

The last step in deliverance is to ask the person to pray that the Holy Spirit will come and fill all places that formerly were occupied by evil spirits. This is an important step. If the Holy Spirit is not invited to fill the places formerly occupied by evil spirits, then the enemy can and will return to those places, oftentimes in a stronger way than before.[3]

When you feel confident that all doors are closed, then you are ready to lead the delivered one in praise and thanksgiving to Jesus for their deliverance. This is a joyful time. Join in with your own thanks and praise.

FOLLOW UP

Even though a person has been delivered, continued healing may be needed in relationships or other areas. John Wimber once remarked to me that deliverance is the easy part. The hard part is helping a person stay free and enter into a healthy relational lifestyle.

Encourage the person who has been delivered to continue to seek prayer and counseling if needed. Also encourage them to walk in a spiritually healthy way by reading their Bible and participating in Christian fellowship, which will help change old lifestyle habits.

LIVING FREE

Any hurts that arise should be acknowledged, forgiven, and given to God right away so that access doors cannot be opened. Explain to them that praising God and praying in their prayer language will help keep access doors closed, and that freedom can be maintained if they allow Jesus into every area of their life. Encourage them to ask the Holy Spirit to come and fill them on a daily basis. If they are willing to take responsibility for their thoughts and walk in forgiveness, they can remain delivered.

Walking in forgiveness must become the lifestyle of every believer who wishes to stay free of bondage. Forgiveness is a decision, not a feeling. We can forgive even when we don't feel forgiveness. Our spirit can rule over our emotions. Sometimes forgiveness is a process and not just a one-time occurrence. We may need to forgive the same person many times. This is not a sign that deliverance ministry was a failure. It is a normal part of the human condition. Forgiveness is in our own best interest.

There are many ways people can change crucial habit patterns that have been destructive in their lives, replacing them with godly habits. They can develop the habit of praising God by singing or listening to praise music, continually thanking Him for setting them free.

Learning to take authority over tempting spirits in the name of Jesus and sending them away is another valuable habit to cultivate. If someone falls, they can repent quickly and close any door that was reopened. If Satan, the accuser of the brethren, tries to torment by reminding a person that they are a sinner, they can reply with: "You're right, Satan. Just look at what Jesus has forgiven me for!"

By cultivating a relationship with the Holy Spirit, every believer can learn how to walk in the light. My friend Rodney Hogue, in his book *Forgiveness*, succinctly examines the issue of rebuilding life with a stronghold of compassion. Rodney explains why and how compassion is the righteous stronghold that gives us the power to sustain forgiveness and stay free.[4]

It is God's will for us that we learn to walk in forgiveness[5] because a heart clothed in love and humility is protected from offense. Just as we have been forgiven, so must we learn to forgive.[6]

Some people may need extensive follow-up in order to be free of lifestyle choices and habits that have come upon them as a result of demonic infestation or possession. This is especially true of those who were involved in satanic activities. The process can be complex and time consuming and should be undertaken with a trained counselor who is skilled in post-deliverance counseling. Be aware that the person will likely require the strong support of family and friends during this process. Becoming part of a Christian cell group or other small relational Christian group is an important step that will enhance their freedom and assist their continued growth in Christ and the process of sanctification.

DELIVERANCE TEAM DYNAMICS

It is important that those of us who minister deliverance are ourselves free of any ungodly bondage or demonic influence and that the ministry team is in unity. If we are not free, we can begin to manifest as we try to minister deliverance to others.

I know a husband and wife in Mozambique who operate in a strong deliverance ministry. People actually line up outside their house and will wait for hours or days, if the couple isn't at home, to receive deliverance. They have had instances in which, during deliverance, those on the ministry team who were not free have begun to manifest in frightening and dangerous ways, such as trying to throw themselves out of second-story windows or undressing. As I have said before, the enemy does not play fair; he will take advantage of every opportunity to steal, kill, and destroy.

In 2001 I was leading a team in Brazil. Our last stop was the small city of Santarém in northern Brazil. Tom Hauser relates this story in his book *Breaking Free*,[7] and I want to share it here with you, as I recall it, because it illustrates the need both for team unity and for all of us to be "cleaned up" before we minister deliverance.

We didn't realize what we were walking into when we arrived in Santarém. The oppression that blanketed the city was palpable. The people there were in the middle of celebrating the Festival of the Dolphins. Immoral sexual behavior was a major part of the celebration. There were even people having sex on the grounds of the hotel when we arrived!

The people believed that during the Festival of the Dolphins, dolphins would manifest as men and have sex with women. Festival time translated into free sex. This kind of behavior over the years had left the city broken and oppressed. Such was the atmosphere we found ourselves in.

Tom Hauser discerned that the best way to begin dealing with the situation was to confront it during the first night of ministry. I was to lead the service that night, and the plan was for me to confront the demonic by taking authority over the spirits.

As we gathered the team to pray before the service, it became apparent that we were not in unity. Some of the team members began to argue. Tom was able to lead all of them through forgiveness except for one woman, who couldn't let go of her anger. When the worship ended, I stood up as planned and, taking authority, bound the witchcraft. Immediately people fell down and began to manifest. It was like a war zone.

As our team began to minister, the woman on the team who had been unable to forgive was beset by a tormenting spirit and passed out. Then one of the other team members was overcome with fear. The unforgiveness and lack of unity had opened a door for the demonic to come in and attack our team. I began ministering to the team member who had passed out, and the woman she couldn't forgive joined me. Together we broke off the tormenting spirit.

This experience became the basis for training our teams in the importance of being "cleaned up" and in unity. I teach team unity in my Empowered School of Healing and Impartation, and Tom Hauser teaches it in his ministry. Today Santarém is a different city. Pastor Abe Huber's church has over fifty thousand people meeting in Christian cell groups all over the city. Once a month new converts participate in a retreat where they go through inner healing and deliverance, and are filled with the Holy Spirit.

POST-DELIVERANCE

Those involved in deliverance ministry should get in the habit of covering themselves and their family members with the blood of Jesus and putting on the full armor of God. After ministering to the demonized, take time to dust off any residue from the encounters. Ask the Lord to wash everything off you, to cancel any assignments of hell, and to release the assignments of heaven over you and your team. Ask Him to keep your mind pure, guard your emotions, protect your body, and bless those who would curse you.

TALKING TO DEMONS

While ministering one night in Belém, Brazil, with the Global team, we encountered demons that tried to talk to us.[8] We were ministering to a young woman. Born into a Macumba witchcraft family, she was forced into prostitution at an early age. She was only fifteen years old when she came to our service for deliverance. Her countenance was tormented.

As I began to minister to her through a translator, she fell to the ground screaming and vomiting blood. We learned that this is not uncommon for those who have eaten food sacrificed to idols during Macumba rituals. We asked her if she wanted to be free from demonic oppression and accept Jesus Christ as her Lord and Savior. She agreed, and we made arrangements for her to return for deliverance ministry the next day.

She showed up the next day, and as the team gathered around her and began to minister to her, the demons began to torment her severely, choking her to the point that she couldn't speak. Because she was unable to confess her sins and ask for forgiveness, we asked the Holy Spirit what to do, and He told us to use "hand-to-hand combat." Knowing we had a battle on our hands, the seven of us linked arms in the spirit and commenced to cast out everything the Holy Spirit brought to mind.

I had to step away, but during the three to four hours that our team ministered to her, she manifested in some very bizarre ways. Many find this hard to believe, but at one point she elevated off the floor like a board even though several team members were sitting on top of her. Then the demons began to speak to them.

In a loud and clear voice and in perfect English one of them spoke to a team member named Mark saying, "I am going to kill you." We knew it couldn't have been the young woman we were ministering to because she spoke only Portuguese. We ignored the demon, and at the leading of the Holy Spirit we prayed in tongues for an extended period of time, after which the demon spoke again saying, "It is getting hot in here!"

Figuring that the fire of the Holy Spirit was literally burning them out, we pressed in, praying in tongues until the demons left her. On the way out they said, "We are leaving!" This young woman was set free, and when we saw her the next day she looked and acted like a normal fifteen-year-old girl.

I do not believe we are to talk to demons during deliverance. I believe this notion that we are to address the demon comes from a misunderstanding of Scripture. In Mark 5 the Word says:

> When he saw Jesus from a distance, he ran and fell on his knees in front of him. He shouted at the top of his voice, "What do you want with me, Jesus, Son of the Most High God? In God's name don't torture me!" For Jesus had said to him, "Come out of this man, you impure spirit!"
>
> —MARK 5:6–8

In this verse it is the demon that is addressing Jesus, not the demonized man. Jesus had already discerned the evil spirit in the man and commanded it to come out. Then, in verse 9, we read:

> Then Jesus asked him, "What is your name?" "My name is Legion," he replied, "for we are many."

This is where I believe more confusion lies. Many interpret this to mean that Jesus is addressing the demon by asking its name. I do not think Jesus was initiating a dialogue with the evil spirit. I think He was asking the man his name, and the demonic spirit answered. Some deliverance models teach that we must know the name of the demon in order to take authority over it. That is not what I teach because, according to the Bible, we already have authority over the demonic.[9]

The ministry of deliverance has not always been characterized by sanity or balance. Guidelines and methods can help bring balance, and it is up to those of us who train and minister deliverance to do so with the utmost compassion and integrity, using Scripture as our basis. The *charismata* are given to enable us to fulfill the Great Commission. We must exercise them with humility and love as we the church advance the kingdom of God in the world. There is much still to be done!

Chapter 14

MOVING FORWARD

＊━━━━◆◆◆◆━━━━＊

I AM PRIVILEGED TO TRAVEL THE WORLD TO bring people the message of the power and authority given to all believers by the finished work of Jesus on the cross. I have witnessed firsthand the kingdom of God pushing back the powers of darkness through ordinary individuals. The authority for deliverance is not just available to a select few in the church. It is available to all believers. Deliverance is the children's bread, a New Testament reality won for us by Jesus on the cross.

I long to see the entire church come into a full understanding of the ministry of deliverance. Jesus came to set the captives free and commissioned us to continue this work in His name. The advance of His kingdom involves a continuing "jail break" for people who have been imprisoned by the devil. When people are set free from entanglement with the enemy, they are able to come into the fullness of who God intends them to be.

162

THE GREAT NEED FOR DELIVERANCE

Much of the church today languishes; it is powerless—caught up in theology that relegates the power of God to the distant past or to the millennial reign in the future or to the consummation of the kingdom of God—with little emphasis placed on the current power of God. Satan would like to keep the church in this weakened state of power position for as long as he can, because when we regain our power, he will quickly find himself with few places to hide.

The early church moved in this power. It was the power—with its accompanying miracles, signs, and wonders—that built the church. When confronted with the power of God to heal the sick, raise the dead, and set the captives free, unbelievers abandoned their pagan practices for the message of the gospel.[1] That same power is available to all believers today.

The power of the Holy Spirit and all the authority of Jesus Christ[2] are available to us as believers today. But so often we fail to understand who we are. We fail to understand our identity in Christ because the church has not taught us who we are. Many in leadership in the church today do not themselves understand the identity of the believer and so they cannot teach it to their flocks.

163

Dr. Pablo Deiros shared with me in 1996 how God highlighted for him the great need for deliverance within the church, starting with leadership. He was ministering deliverance to a Southern Baptist missionary who had been in the field for forty years. The man and his wife had been struggling for years with the husband's sins, which were preventing him from serving the Lord in freedom.

They were unable to live in the fullness of Christ or to flow in the power of the Holy Spirit because of his sin. The man would avoid situations in which he would need to minister in the power of the Spirit because whenever he had tried to minister that way, the devil had come along and reminded him of his own sin.

The encounter opened Dr. Deiros's eyes to the great need in the church for deliverance for clergy and their spouses. He estimates that in Argentina approximately 80 percent of pastors were raped or abused as children, with the numbers increasing slightly for female pastors. He found similar statistics when ministering in Chile.

How can the church grow and be renewed and filled with the Holy Spirit and the gifts of the Spirit if its leadership is struggling under such a burden? The Lord wants to clean and embellish His bride, and He must begin with the leadership. The sheep of the flock cannot be healed and set free if their leaders are not walking in freedom.

Dr. Deiros set up clinics to meet the need for healing and deliverance for clergy—and they came by the hundreds to be healed and restored so they might return to their churches with new vision and motivation. They not only were delivered, but they also were trained in deliverance so they could take it back to their churches. Dr. Deiros and his team also brought these clinics to Chile and the United States.

Another outgrowth of his awareness of the need for training were the many programs that were instituted in local churches in Argentina to train the laity in deliverance ministry. Just as we train both clergy and laity in the United States in areas such as evangelism, preaching, and teaching, so they train clergy and laity in Argentina how to minister deliverance.

In many churches in Argentina you will find well-trained teams of men and women ready to assist people who manifest. If someone begins to manifest the demonic in a regular church service, ushers know immediately how to handle the situation. They quietly assist the person out of the sanctuary to a private place where trained counselors are waiting.

It is a normal part of the church's life—as normal as collecting the offering. People in the congregation are not surprised or disturbed because they are confident that the situation will be handled tactfully, with respect and love, and because they have come to understand the value of deliverance.

After the disciples were "clothed" with the Spirit at Pentecost, they went out from Jerusalem and, in the power of the Spirit, took the good news into the world, pushing back the work of the devil with the kingdom of God. We can do the same today.

In the New Testament we find Paul dealing with a sorcerer. Notice that he did not wade into the battle unarmed. He was filled with the Holy Spirit:

> Then Saul, who also is called Paul, filled with the Holy Spirit, stared at him and said, "You son of the devil, enemy of all righteousness, full of deceit and of all fraud, will you not cease perverting the right ways of the Lord? Now, look! The hand of the Lord is against you, and you shall be blind, not seeing the sun for a time." Immediately mist and darkness fell on him, and he went about seeking someone to lead him by the hand.
>
> —ACTS 13:9–11, MEV

In this passage Paul is addressing the sorcerer so that he might understand the truth of the gospel, and he is also addressing the demon. His words are harsh, but this is a power encounter with the enemy. Notice that the scripture tells us that the blindness was only temporary. The end of this story is not harsh, though. It is an expression of God's love. Just as Saul's (Paul's) blindness resulted in him coming to an understanding of the truth of who Jesus is, so the proconsul in this story is brought into the light. "When the proconsul saw what had happened, he believed, for he was amazed at the teaching about the Lord" (Acts 13:12).

DELIVERANCE: AN EXPRESSION OF GOD'S LOVE

We are made in God's image.[3] He delights in us. So great is His love for us that He sent His only Son to die in our place. Jesus says we are the salt of the earth,[4] the light of the world.[5] We are seated with Him in heavenly places. We are his workmanship, created in Christ to do the works that God prepared for us in advance (Eph. 2:6–7, 10).

I have been privileged to learn so much over the years about deliverance thanks to those who came alongside me and taught me what it means to set the captives free with the love of Christ. I believe the ministry of deliverance is a "love" ministry. Darren Wilson calls it "furious love" in his documentary film by the same name about the power and love of God.[6] God's authority can be furious—swift and intense and energetic—but He is the God of love.

Make no mistake, we will not just encounter the devil and his demons outside the walls of the church in some faraway third world country. He is active and at work within the church everywhere, and we need to be equipped to deal with him. Deliverance belongs to the church, as a part of the process of sanctification. The ministry of deliverance should not have been lost to the church. It is a vital part of the advance of God's kingdom, and it is necessary if we are to walk in freedom.

My friend SoPhal Ung, a Cambodian pastor, has seen evil up close many times in his life.[7] And just as often, he has seen the power of God overcome evil. A native Cambodian, born a Buddhist in a predominantly Buddhist country, SoPhal came to Christ as a young man just as Cambodia entered one of the darkest periods in its history. Genocide on par with the Holocaust ravaged Cambodia, leaving the country bleeding and broken. Amid the most unimaginable evil the light of God pushed back the darkness in Cambodia through people like SoPhal who stood on the authority of Christ every day at the risk of their lives.

SoPhal endured imprisonment, torture, starvation, and near death in places so dark and deep it was almost impossible for him to imagine how the light of Christ could find him. Yet it did.

In his darkest moment he remembered the story of Paul and Silas singing in prison, and so he too sang into the darkness. He was actually preaching as he sang "River of Life." Those around him began to sing with him. Over time almost every person in that filthy prison gave their life to Christ before they died. Of the hundreds who were imprisoned with SoPhal, all but two perished. Heaven is populated today with those dear ones because one man understood the authority of Jesus Christ for all believers.

The Bible tells us that Satan is doomed[8] and that the fire of God will come down from heaven and devour the devil and his demons even as they march across the breadth of the earth and surround the camp of God's people. Until Christ's glorious return, we are to remember that He who is in us is greater than he who is in the world,[9] for we are more than conquerors in Christ Jesus.

AFTERWORD

I WANT TO END THIS BOOK ON THE MINISTRY OF deliverance by bringing our focus back to Jesus, our deliverer. Satan and his demons know exactly who Jesus is and so must we. Born as God in the flesh into a world that understood and demanded an earthly king, one to rule them all, Jesus came as our heavenly King, bringing with Him heaven to earth.

This book, like most books on the ministry of deliverance, has focused a great deal on an understanding of Satan. Those called to the ministry of deliverance must have a firm grasp of who Satan is and the many ways in which he operates in order to minister effectively. But it is not our knowledge of Satan nor how skillfully we apply it that we bring to those who are struggling, caught in Satan's web of deceit and destruction. As we look into the faces of those we minister to, we must offer them Jesus, our deliverer, for there is no one that can bring freedom from the bondage of Satan except our matchless King, Jesus Christ. When we shine the light of Christ into the darkness of bondage and despair, His light overcomes all darkness. Understanding our enemy is key to the battle, but understanding the One who brings victory is how the battle is won.

The world was seething with unrest, violence, brutality and darkness when Jesus broke upon the scene. God's chosen people, the Jews, had been longing for the Messiah promised by the prophets for centuries. This Messiah would deliver them from their enemies and establish His reign, and the people of God would find safety and prosperity in His earthly kingdom. The prophet Isaiah spoke of the one who would bind up the brokenhearted, proclaim freedom for the captives and release from darkness for the prisoners.[1] His words resonated with the Jewish people who had struggled under the yoke of captivity and oppression for generations. They didn't understand that Isaiah was prophesying of a heavenly king whose rule from heaven would change the earth.

At the time of Jesus's birth the Jewish people were under the control the Roman Empire, ruled by Herod the Great, a cruel and ruthless right-hand man to Augustus Caesar. Herod's brutality knew no bounds. Executions were commonplace and numerous and included Herod's own wife, who was put to death at his command, as were two of his sons. Human life had little value. Human sacrifice was rare but still practiced at times for spiritual purposes.

Every aspect of Jewish life was impacted by Roman rule. Struggling mightily to remain the people of God, Jewish nationalistic opposition took many forms. The Zealot movement opposed all things Roman, while the Sadducees sought coexistence and were allowed by the Romans to rule an internal government for the Jewish nation. The Pharisees practiced strict adherence to Jewish law in the hopes of hastening the coming of the long-awaited Messiah.

The culture surrounding the Jewish people was religiously pluralistic. The Romans and Greeks worshipped multiple gods, and paganism was rampant. The city of Corinth, like most major cities in the region, seethed with unbound immorality. Temples dedicated to Greek gods filled Corinth. Those who worshipped Aphrodite, the goddess of love, practiced prostitution in the name of religion, with hundreds of "sacred" prostitutes serving at the temple.

Against this backdrop the Jewish people longed for their Messiah, the conquering king who would liberate them from Roman rule and establish justice and peace. God brought them the promised Messiah, but Jesus's birth, life, death, and resurrection were so unlike what they had expected that they failed to recognize Him. The conquering King with a sword in hand and a throne to sit upon didn't materialize in Jesus of Nazareth in ways that the people expected.

CHRIST THE DELIVERER

The world at the time of Jesus's birth was not unlike the world today. Corruption, immorality, greed, lust, brutality, and godlessness still live in the hearts of men. And many of us fail to see that our promised Messiah has come.

I believe it is in the ministry of healing and deliverance that we are most able to see Jesus today. It is when the blind see, the lame walk, the deaf hear, the dead are raised that we see Jesus bring His kingdom to bear on the earth, as well as the ministry to the poor done in His name. When demons are cast out of a person in the name of Jesus, and that person is restored to his right mind and able to live as God created him to live, we are seeing Jesus wield His sword from His throne at the right hand of God.

When we minister deliverance in the authority of Jesus Christ, spiritual bondage gives way to the kingdom of heaven because Satan and his demons know that all authority in the spiritual realm rests with Jesus Christ and Him alone.[2] And Jesus Himself commissions us with this authority.[3] We can bear no fruit outside of Jesus.[4]

After His temptation in the wilderness Jesus returned to Nazareth, to the synagogue, on the Sabbath day. The scroll of the prophet Isaiah was handed to Him as He stood to read. With the words of Isaiah 61 He declared His identity: "The Spirit of the Sovereign LORD is on me, because the LORD has anointed me to proclaim good news to the poor. He has sent me to bind up the brokenhearted, to proclaim freedom for the captives and release from darkness for the prisoners, to proclaim the year of the LORD's favor" (vv. 1–2).

A great light had come to shine upon a people walking in darkness. A child had been born, a son given. And the government was to be upon *His* shoulders. And He was to be called, Wonderful Counselor, Mighty God, Everlasting Father, Prince of Peace. There will be no end to the increase of His government and peace, and He will rule with justice and righteousness forever.[5]

This is Jesus who saw Satan and his fallen angels cast out of heaven.[6] This is Jesus who rose from the grave and ascended into heaven to sit at the right hand of the Father.[7] This is Jesus who has absolute control over death and hell through His resurrection.[8] This is Jesus of the Gospels who went about healing and delivering. Storms calmed in His presence, food multiplied, and water turned to wine. Leprosy, paralysis, bleeding, blindness, deafness, and withered limbs were healed. The dead were raised. Demons fled at His command. Those in bondage to the demonic were set free by the word of His mouth.

This is the Jesus of the gospel that Paul proclaimed, the Jesus that, "...having disarmed the powers and authorities, he made a public spectacle of them, triumphing over them by the cross" (Col. 2:15).

The powers and authorities here are referring to spiritual evil powers and authorities. The public spectacle refers to how conquering Roman generals would often return to Rome after battle. When possible they would drag the defeated general of the opposing army, hands tied to his chariot, all his regalia stripped away, naked, exposing him to public humiliation as the defeated one. This is the picture Paul is referencing in Colossians 2:15. Jesus is the conquering general of the Lord's heavenly host, which outnumbers the fallen demons two to one. He is also the captain of our faith (Heb. 2:10, KJV) and the head of the church (Eph. 5:23).

If you have ministered healing and deliverance, you know that these same things are happening today. Jesus continues to heal and set the captives free. As humanity groans and thrashes about in the midst of our sin, we have a deliverer, and His name is Jesus. The ministry of deliverance advances the kingdom of God in the world, and that is why Satan fights so hard against it. He has tried to keep the church tied up in spasms of confusion over the reality of evil for centuries, but he has not fully succeeded nor will he ever because Jesus is alive.

When we understand that freedom equates to advancement, and appropriate that understanding into ministry, God will use us to bring the reality of His incomparable Son Jesus Christ to the lost and broken. Even one deliverance can impact the world for all time. Take for instance the apostle Paul. Paul experienced deliverance in the midst of his conversion. A rabid antagonist of Christianity, with a slavish devotion to Jewish law, Saul's (Paul's) passion was to eradicate the followers of Jesus thereby destroying the fledgling church. He went about his mission with great zeal. He gave approval for the death of Stephen[9] and took part in inciting the crowd to begin to rise up and persecute the church in Jerusalem. "But Saul began to destroy the church. Going from house to house, he dragged off men and women and put them in prison" (Acts 8:3).

With murderous threats on his lips he set out for Damascus with letters of authority to round up Christians and bring them to trial when suddenly, in a moment of encounter with Jesus, Saul's life was forever changed. Called out by name for his sins against believers, Saul was blinded by Jesus on the road to Damascus. For three days he was blind, until a man of God placed his hands upon him and in the name of Jesus his eyes were opened. As the scales fell from his physical eyes, filled with the Holy Spirit, Saul was able to see the truth of the gospel.

Saul became Paul and the work of building the church that had begun with the disciples extended to this man who was once bent on its destruction. Paul's slavish adherence to the law as the way to salvation was replaced with a personal knowledge of the living Jesus Christ. The spiritual chains that bound Saul were broken by the power of Jesus, not with earthly power and might, but with heavenly power.

Paul's ministry was characterized by healings and deliverances as he went about the work of advancing the church throughout the Roman Empire and beyond. The extraordinary miracles that Paul performed in the power of the Holy Spirit became quite well known,[10] so much so that imitators began to spring up. The seven sons of Sceva attempted to cast out demons "in the name of Jesus, whom Paul preaches..." but the evil spirits recognized them as imposters without power and did not obey them.[11]

As believers in Jesus Christ and ministers of the gospel we are not imposters. We are God's beloved, and

He has given us His Son so that not even one may perish. We are to be imitators of Christ, taking His kingdom boldly into those dark places that need the light of His presence. We are to be a new covenant people. "'As for me, this is my covenant with them,' says the LORD. 'My Spirit, who is on you, will not depart from you, and my words that I have put in your mouth will always be on your lips, on the lips of your children and on the lips of their descendants—from this time on and forever,' says the LORD" (Isa. 59:21).

God's second act of creation, after creating the heavens and the earth, was to bring light to the darkness. He is the Father of Lights and He has given us the light of the world in Jesus. "Every good and perfect gift is from above, coming down from the Father of the heavenly lights, who does not change like shifting shadows. He chose to give us birth through the word of truth, that we might be a kind of firstfruits of all he created" (James 1:17–18). When we proclaim the gospel through the ministry of healing and deliverance, we are proclaiming that the whole harvest will eventually follow. Jesus is the Lord of the harvest and through Him we are invited to become participants.

As you minister healing and deliverance to the broken and the lost, remember the words of Heidi Baker, who says, "Love looks like something."[12] She is telling us that love looks like Jesus, the suffering servant, the One despised and rejected by men, a man of sorrows, and One familiar with suffering. The One who took our infirmities, the One pierced for our transgressions, crushed for our iniquities, who bore the iniquity of us all so that we could be set free. His love does not delight in evil, but always rejoices with the truth, always protects, always trusts, always hopes, always perseveres.[13] This is our mandate for the ministry of deliverance—no, for the ministry of the whole gospel, until Jesus returns.

NOTES

INTRODUCTION

1. F. F. Bosworth, *Christ the Healer* (Grand Rapids, MI: Chosen, 2008), 179.

2. Ibid., 74.

3. Randy Clark, *There Is More!* (Grand Rapids, MI: Chosen, 2013), 102.

4. Ibid., 103–104.

5. Hughes Oliphant Old, *The Shaping of the Reformed Baptismal Rite in the Sixteenth Century* (Grand Rapids, MI: Wm. B. Eerdmans Publishing Co., 1992). This book offers an in-depth study of the history of baptism in the early church.

6. Laurence W. Wood, *The Meaning of Pentecost in Early Methodism* (Lanham, MD: Scarecrow Press, 2002), 358.

7. *Constitutions of the Holy Apostles* Book VII, Sec. III—On the Instruction of Catechumens, and Their Initiation Into Baptism. (Kindle Edition, 2013).

8. Ryan C. MacPherson, "A History of the Baptismal Order: From the Early Church Through the Lutheran Reformation, to Contemporary Rites," http://www.ryancmacpherson.com /publication-list/26-research-papers/90-a-history-of-the -baptismal-order.html (accessed December 27, 2014).

9. Ibid.

10. Ibid.; Philip H. Pfatteicher, *Commentary on the Lutheran Book of Worship: Lutheran Liturgy in Its Ecumenical Context* (Minneapolis, MN: Augsburg Fortress Press, 1990), 47.

11. *The Book of Common Prayer and the Administration of the Sacraments and Other Rites and Ceremonies of the Church* (New York: The Church Hymnal Corporation, 1979).

12. Ibid., 415–419.

13. Brian Cummings, ed., *The Book of Common Prayer* (Oxford, England: Oxford University Press, 2011).

14. Healing of the Spirit Ministries, "About Healing of the Spirit Ministries," http://healingofthespirit.org/aboutus.html (accessed December 26, 2014).

15. Pablo Bottari, *Free in Christ* (Lake Mary, FL: Charisma House, 2000), 65–139.

16. Francis MacNutt, *Deliverance From Evil Spirits* (Grand Rapids, MI: Chosen Books, 1995, 2009).

17. Neal Lozano, *Unbound* (Grand Rapids, MI: Chosen Books, 2003, 2010).

18. James W. Goll, *Deliverance From Darkness: The Essential Guide to Defeating Demonic Strongholds and Oppression* (Grand Rapids, MI: Chosen Books, 2010).

19. Malachi Martin, *Hostage to the Devil: The Possession and Exorcism of Five Contemporary Americans* (San Francisco: HarperSanFrancisco, 1992).

20. Walter Wink, *Naming the Powers: The Language of Power in the New Testament* (Minneapolis, MN: Fortress Press, 1984); *Unmasking the Powers: The Invisible Forces That Determine Human Existence* (Minneapolis, MN: Fortress Press, 1986); *Engaging the Powers: Discernment and Resistance in a World of Domination* (Minneapolis, MN: Fortress Press, 1992).

21. Tuol Sleng Museum of Genocide; Phnom Penh, Cambodia.

22. Wulf Schwarzwaeller, *The Unknown Hitler* (New York: Berkley Books, 1990).

23. Nicholas Goodrick-Clarke, *The Occult Roots of Nazism* (New York: NYU Press, 1993).

24. John Paul Jackson, *Needless Casualties of War* (Fort Worth, TX: Streams Publications, 1999).

CHAPTER 1
MY INTRODUCTION TO DELIVERANCE

1. Bottari, *Free in Christ*.
2. The names in this story have been changed to protect the privacy of those involved.

CHAPTER 2
DELIVERANCE: A NEW TESTAMENT REALITY

1. See Romans 16:20.
2. See Romans 8:37–39.
3. See Matthew 12:24.
4. See John 8:44.
5. See John 11:14.
6. See Acts 5:3.
7. See 2 Corinthians 11:14–15.
8. See Ephesians 2:2.
9. See Acts 13:4–12.
10. See Matthew 24:11, 24.
11. See Acts 8:9–25.
12. See 2 Corinthians 2:11.
13. 2 Corinthians 4:4.
14. Hebrews 2:14.
15. See 2 Timothy 2:26.
16. See 1 Peter 5:8.
17. See 1 Corinthians 7:5.
18. See 1 Corinthians 10:19–21.
19. See Matthew 4:1–11; Mark 1; Luke 4:1–13.
20. See Luke 13:16.
21. See Luke 10:17.
22. See Mark 1:23–24.
23. See Mark 5:1–20.
24. See Acts 10:38.

25. See Ephesians 4:26–27.
26. See Ephesians 6:10–18.
27. John 8:44.
28. See John 13:2; 13:27.
29. Revelation 12:8–9; 20:2.

CHAPTER 3
THE THEOLOGY OF DELIVERANCE

1. See Matthew 14:14; Romans 15:18–19.
2. Craig Keener, *Miracles: The Credibility of the New Testament Accounts* (Grand Rapids, MI: Baker Academic, 2011), 849.
3. Matthew 6:10.

CHAPTER 4
DELIVERANCE IN THE HISTORY OF THE CHURCH

1. Morton T. Kelsey, *Healing and Christianity* (New York: Harper and Row, 1973, 1976), 136 (Kelsey references: Justin Martyr; Second Apology to the Roman Senate 6: see the Anti-Nicene Fathers).
2. Ibid., 136–151.
3. Ibid., 152.
4. Eddie L. Hyatt, *2000 Years of Charismatic Christianity* (Lake Mary, FL: Charisma House, 2002), 38–39.
5. Leon Joseph Cardinal Suenens, *A New Pentecost?* (New York: Seabury, 1975), in Hyatt, *2000 Years of Charismatic Christianity*, 38.
6. Hyatt, *2000 Years of Charismatic Christianity*, 39.
7. Ibid.; Athanasius, *Life of Antony*, vol. 4 of *Nicene and Post-Nicene Fathers of the Christian Church*, 200.
8. Hyatt, *2000 Years of Charismatic Christianity*, 44.
9. Ibid.
10. Ibid., 74–75.

11. Roberts Liardon, *God's Generals* (New Kensington, PA: Whitaker House, 2008), 61.

12. Ibid., 61.

13. Ibid., 62.

14. Hyatt, *2000 Years of Charismatic Christianity*, 102.

15. Liardon, *God's Generals*, 284.

16. Charles Finney, "The Christian Warfare," *The Oberlin Evangelist*, March 1, 1843, http://www.spiritualwarfare deliverance.com/classics-christian-warfare-deliverance-healing /html/christian-warfare-by-finney.html (accessed January 30, 2015).

17. Ibid.

18. Lester Sumrall, *Demons: The Answer Book* (New Kensington, PA: Whitaker House, 1979), 11–25. This story can also be viewed on the web at http://www.youtube.com/watch ?v=SKwUui-ei7E (accessed December 27, 2014).

19. Lester Sumrall, "Evangelism, Healing, and Deliverance," Healing and Revival Press, http://healingandrevival.com /BioLSumrall.htm (accessed December 27, 2014).

CHAPTER 5
CAN A CHRISTIAN BE DEMONIZED?

1. See Matthew 12:44–45.

CHAPTER 6
SIGNS OF DEMONIZATION

1. Luke 13:11–13.
2. John 10:10.

Chapter 7
Deliverance as Part of the
Process of Sanctification

1. Regent University School of Divinity, "Vinson Synan," http://www.regent.edu/acad/schdiv/faculty/synan/ (accessed December 27, 2014).

2. As quoted in Kenneth J. Collins, *John Wesley: A Theological Journey* (Nashville: Abingdon Press, 2003).

3. "Whosoever committeth sin transgresseth also the law: for sin is the transgression of the law" (1 John 3:4, KJV).

4. "But the person who does anything with a high hand ["defiantly," NIV; "presumptuously," KJV], whether he is native or a sojourner, reviles the LORD, and that person shall be cut off from among his people. Because he has despised the word of the LORD, and has broken his commandment, that person shall be utterly cut off; his iniquity shall be upon him" (Num. 15:30–31, RSV).

Chapter 8
Curses, Inner Vows, Soul Ties, and
Generational Curses

1. Derek Prince, *Blessing or Curse: You Can Choose* (Grand Rapids, MI: Chosen Books, 2006).

2. Ibid., 53.

3. Ibid.

4. Ibid., 68.

5. See Galatians 3:13; Ephesians 4:29.

Chapter 9
Satan and Demons

1. See Isaiah 14:12–18.

2. See Luke 10:18.

3. See Revelation 12:9.
4. See Ephesians 2:6.
5. See Revelation 5:11.
6. See Colossians 1:27.
7. See Ephesians 4:27.
8. See Matthew 25:34.
9. See Matthew 25:41.

CHAPTER 10
THE OCCULT AND DEMONIZATION

1. *Strong's Expanded Exhaustive Concordance of the Bible* (Nashville: Thomas Nelson Publishers, 2010).

2. This is a partial list of scriptures that address occult practices: Deuteronomy 4:19, 17:2–5; 2 Kings 21:3, 5; Job 31:26–28; Isaiah 47:10–14; Jeremiah 8:1–2; 10:2; 27:9–10; Daniel 2:1–4, 4:7, 5:7–9; Zephaniah 1:5, Acts 13:7–10; 16:16–18; 19:19; Galatians 5:19–20; Revelation 22:15.

3. Come and Hear, "Blood Ritual," http://www.come-and-hear.com/editor/br_3.html (accessed February 2, 2015).

4. Jack R. Lundbom, *Deuteronomy: A Commentary* (Grand Rapids, MI: Wm. B. Eerdmans Publishing, 2013), 439–440.

5. Kenneth Barker, ed., *The NIV Study Bible, 10th Anniversary Edition* (Grand Rapids, MI: Zondervan, 1995), 1687.

6. Randy Clark and Susan Thompson, *Healing Energy: Whose Is It?* (Mechanicsburg, PA: Global Awakening, 2013), 59; Sharon Fish, "Therapeutic Touch," Christian Research Institute, http://www.equip.org/articles/therapeutic-touch/ (accessed December 27, 2014).

7. Ibid.

8. Ibid., 60; Partap Khalsa and John Killen Jr., "'Reiki': An Introduction," National Center for Complementary and

Alternative Medicine, http://nccam.nih.gov/health/reiki/introduction.htm#hed6 (accessed December 27, 2014).

9. Clark and Thompson, *Healing Energy*, 65.

10. This book can be ordered from Global Awakening online at http://globalawakeningstore.com.

11. Eternal Word Television Network, "Jesus Christ, the Bearer of the Water of Life," http://www.ewtn.com/library/CURIA/PCCPCIDA.HTM (accessed December 27, 2014).

12. Ibid.

13. See 2 Corinthians 11:14.

CHAPTER 11
FREEMASONRY

1. Tom Hauser, *Breaking Free* (Shippensburg, PA: Destiny Image, 2012), 98.

2. Barbara Cassada, *Unto Death* (Maryville, TN: Tome Publishing, 2007), 22. Can be ordered through Global Awakening's bookstore online at http://globalawakeningstore.com.

3. Ibid., 22–23.

4. Ibid.

5. To download his manual, go to http://www.healingofthespirit.org/ministry.html.

6. Cassada, *Unto Death*, 9.

7. See Exodus 23:13.

8. Cassada, *Unto Death*, 30.

9. Ibid., 31–22.

10. Ibid., 60–62.

11. Ibid., 62.

12. Ibid., 44–56. This prayer model has been taken and adapted from *Unmasking Freemasonry* by S. Stevens; it is used with permission.

13. In personal communication with the author.

CHAPTER 12
MINISTERING DELIVERANCE

1. See Luke 9:1–2; 10:1, 9; John 14:12; 1 Corinthians 2.

2. See Romans 8:38–39; Matthew 28:18; Ephesians 1:21–22.

3. See 2 Kings 6:15–18.

4. See Luke 10:18–20; 2 Corinthians 5:17; Ephesians 1; 2:6; 1 John 2:6; 1 John 5:13.

5. Randy Clark, *Empowered: A School of Healing and Impartation Workbook* (Mechanicsburg, PA: Global Awakening, 2012), 111.

6. Bottari, *Free in Christ*, 20–21.

7. Ibid., xi.

CHAPTER 13
GUIDELINES FOR MINISTERING DELIVERANCE

1. Bottari, *Free in Christ*, 56.

2. In 2 Corinthians 2 Paul is also highlighting the necessity of forgiveness as a way to prevent Satan from outwitting us: "For we are not unaware of his schemes."

3. See Matthew 12:43–44.

4. Rodney Hogue, *Forgiveness* (Hayward, CA: Community of Grace, 2008), 58. This book can be ordered through Global Awakening at http://globalawakeningstore.com.

5. See Matthew 5:38–41.

6. See Colossians 3:13; Ephesians 4:32.

7. Hauser, *Breaking Free*, 54–56.

8. Ibid., 72–74. Tom relates this story in his book, and because I was there I too remember it clearly.

9. Matthew 10:8; Mark 16:17; Luke 9:1, 10:17.

CHAPTER 14
MOVING FORWARD

1. Ramsay MacMullen, *Christianizing the Roman Empire A.D. 100–400* (New Haven and London: Yale University Press, 1984).

2. See Matthew 28:18.

3. See Genesis 1:27.

4. See Matthew 5:13.

5. See Matthew 5:14.

6. *Furious Love*, directed by Darren Wilson (Elgin, IL: Wanderlust Productions, 2010), DVD.

7. The testimony of SoPhal Ung is soon to be published in book form.

8. See Revelation 20:7–10.

9. See 1 John 4:4.

AFTERWORD

1. See Isaiah 61:1.

2. See Matthew 28:18.

3. See Mark 16:15–18.

4. See Matthew 7:22–23.

5. See Isaiah 9:6–8.

6. See Luke 10:18

7. See Acts 2:33

8. See Revelation 1:18

9. See Acts 8:1

10. See Acts 16:18; 19:11.

11. See Acts 19:13–16.

12. Heidi and Rolland Baker, *Learning to Love* (Bloomington, MN: Chosen Books, 2013).

13. See 1 Corinthians 13:6–7.

EMPOWERED
A SCHOOL OF HEALING AND IMPARTATION

"In our Empowered Conferences, thousands of people from all different backgrounds have stepped into supernatural dimensions of healing, deliverance and Holy Spirit empowered ministry. Our School of Healing and Impartation will be an exciting time of equipping, impartation and demonstration. Don't miss out on what could be one of the most significant spiritual experiences of your life!"

Dr. Randy Clark

VISIT GLOBALAWAKENING.COM/EVENTS
FOR MORE INFO

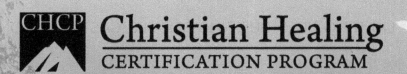